to know
GOD

small-group experiences for spiritual formation

to know
GOD

MICHAEL GEMIGNANI

judson press
VALLEY FORGE

Library of Congress Cataloging-in-Publication Data
Gemignani, Michael C.
    To know God : small group exercises for spiritual formation / Michael
Gemignani.
        p. cm.
    ISBN 0-8170-1394-6 (pbk. : alk. paper)
    1. Spiritual formation. 2. Church group work. 3. Small groups—Religious
aspects—Christianity. I. Title.

BV4511 .G45 2000
248—dc21
                                                                00-050709

Printed in Canada
07 06 05 04 03 02 01

10 9 8 7 6 5 4 3 2 1

*To the people
of St. Paul's Episcopal Church,
Freeport, Texas*

CONTENTS

part three

\

INTRODUCTION

SEVERAL YEARS AGO I ISSUED A CHALLENGE TO MY SMALL CON-gregation. I noted that many persons employed by a local company would jump at the chance to train for an important and highly paid executive position, even if that training extended over several years and required long hours every week. I stated that I had a program that would last only one year and would not require an extensive amount of their time, but if they stayed with the program, their lives would be changed. They would develop a deeper relationship with God and would lay the foundation for continuing spiritual growth.

I felt confident in making this offer because I believe that God will bless richly anyone who makes a firm commitment to say yes to the invitation to enter into the life of God, and who will open himself or herself to the transforming work that God will carry out in those who allow it.

Fifteen people took me up on my offer, and by the end of the year only two had dropped out, both of them for reasons having nothing to do with the program. All who finished felt that their time had been well spent and that God had blessed them. Most stayed on for a second year of the program, and we began to engage in group spiritual direction soon thereafter.

This book is a polished and condensed version of that year-long program I first offered and have offered several times in various forms to others since then. I genuinely believe, based on my experience in giving this program—but primarily because of God's promises to let us grow into spiritual maturity through abundant grace if we will be open to that grace—that those who engage in this program with an open mind and a seeking heart will find it one of the most worthwhile experiences of their lives.

Part One is intended to build a foundation, both theoretical and practical, for the small-group sessions that follow. It addresses various principles, attitudes, and goals related to achieving spiritual growth, and contains practical information related to small-group dynamics and principles of small-group organization.

Part Two, the twelve small-group sessions, comprises the "meat" of this resource. Each session contains questions for individual reflection and group discussion, as well as insights related to the specific topic at hand.

Part Three explores how a group can make the transition from being a short-term spiritual formation group to becoming a long-term spiritual direction group. It also offers material that, if needed, can help spark conversation in response to the additional questions for discussion found in each of the twelve sessions (the comments in this material are my brief reflections and are not intended to be taken as the "right" answers, much less as complete summaries of what might be said.)

May God complete with inspiration and grace all that is lacking in what I have written. I pray that in your efforts to become more open to God's overwhelming love, you will come to a deeper realization of that love which will forever transform your life.

PART ONE

SOME BASIC IDEAS AND THE SMALL-GROUP PROCESS
spiritual formation and spiritual growth

CURRENT RESEARCH INDICATES THAT A LARGE MAJORITY OF Americans are interested in spirituality. At the same time, statistics show that, as a general rule, mainline denominations are declining or barely holding their own numerically, while suffering an overall decline as a percentage of the total population. We may conclude, therefore, that Americans, if they are finding spirituality at all, are finding it with increasing frequency outside the confines of "organized" religion.

I will not conjecture where, or even whether, mainline denominations have failed to provide opportunities for spiritual growth in ways that many of those who claim to seek such growth find attractive. It may be that many do not even examine mainline Christianity because they conclude, for whatever reason, that it has nothing that could interest them. Moreover, the unusual is often more attractive than what is deemed to be familiar. Meditation techniques of Zen Buddhism or the sweat lodge of the Native American may provoke greater interest simply because they are more exotic than the church on the corner.

And yet, the tradition of Western Christianity, not to mention that of Eastern Orthodoxy, is rich in means by which many over the centuries have successfully immersed themselves more fully in the life and mystery of God. Indeed, to immerse oneself in the life of God is the goal of each and every Christian. Scripture and the writings of the most orthodox of theologians tell us no less. "Now we see as through a glass darkly, but then we shall see [God] face to face." "God became a human being, so that human beings could become God."

Thus, the goal of Christian spirituality, however we define it or in whatever form we practice it, is union with God. We can phrase this goal in a variety of ways—for example, to come to know God as God knows us; to become one with Christ and thereby become one with the Father. However we express it, the basic idea is that we are to achieve union with God in love, and through that union to know God as God knows us.

The same research that documents Americans' interest in things spiritual reveals that Americans want the experience of God. They have little use for knowledge about God, that is, theology. As many ministers, myself included, have found to their sorrow, their congregations are becoming more and more theologically illiterate. Many Christians will associate with any denomination that meets their perceived personal and familial needs, with little regard for that denomination's credo. As one of my colleagues, who has a growing congregation, remarked, "This could be a Buddhist temple and they would still come if we had a good program for the children and an entertaining service." This may have been a cynical overstatement, but unfortunately, it contains more than a grain of truth.

Nevertheless, we may safely say that if the goal of Christianity is to come to the knowledge of God, and if this is indeed what Americans hunger for, then denominations must find methods to help people satisfy their hunger. Such methods must be founded on sound Christian principles and the experience of the past, drawing on the best teachings of those recognized as authorities on the spiritual life. The history of Christian spirituality is replete with such methods, many of which are accessible to the average layperson. One does not have to enter an ashram or a monastery to open one's life to God's transforming love.

the essence of spiritual practice

I offer four principles as the foundation of any spiritual practice:

Principle 1: God has invited each and every human being to share in God's own life and to know God personally and intimately, as God knows us.

Principle 2: We cannot come to this knowledge of God through our own efforts, no matter how naturally gifted we may be. We can come to this knowledge only through the action of God.

Principle 3: By our free choice, we can accept the invitation to share in God's life and come to the knowledge of God; likewise, we are free to reject this invitation.

Principle 4: Once we have accepted the invitation, we must open ourselves to allow the Spirit to act in us to bring us to the knowledge of God.

Coming to the knowledge of God is a process. Our spiritual journey begins by accepting God's invitation. The acceptance sets us on the path to spiritual progress, but the goal is generally still far off.

Once we have said yes to God, once we have said that we want to belong completely to God, that we want to be brought into God's own life, that is when we must find some means of opening ourselves to transforming grace; we must adopt some method of intentionally, consciously, and continually yielding ourselves so that the Spirit can complete in us the work that only God can do. But this method of opening ourselves to God must suit our particular temperament and circumstances.

This book presents one such method. This method, based on traditional spiritual practices and theology, has been tested and refined with a number of groups over several years. Certainly, it is not the only method by which a person can open himself or herself to God. For some users, it may not even be a "good" method, good in the sense that it enables them to be more available to God and to discern more clearly how God is acting in their lives so that they can better cooperate with God. But it has, by the testimony of almost all who have stayed with it, served as a framework within which they have been able to make spiritual progress. Indeed, a strong case can be made that any method that is likely to lead to spiritual growth requires structure, commitment, and discipline.

structure, commitment, and discipline

Someone admitted to an undergraduate program typically has four years of study prior to receiving a degree. The choice of a major is open, and within the context of most majors there is a wide choice of electives. The times of day the student will study, whether to live on campus or off campus, how often to eat pizza—all are matters with respect to which the student can exercise a great deal of discretion. But receiving the degree depends on whether the student can satisfactorily complete the work demanded by the faculty. A brilliant student may be able to coast through school, partying much of the time, while a less academically gifted student may have to spend long hours plodding through notes and textbooks with little time for recreation.

The collegiate environment itself imposes some structure for the student—a schedule of classes, assignments to complete by certain deadlines, examinations on specific subject matter at specific times. The student must also have some commitment to learn, a minimal routine that makes study possible, and a modest amount of discipline that enables the learning of what is needed to pass. Lacking those, the student is unlikely to obtain the sought-after degree.

Our spiritual journey, likewise, is not likely to achieve its potential if we lack structure, commitment, and discipline. There are, however, critical differences between the college student seeking his degree and the seeker on a quest to love God with all her heart and mind and soul and strength. The student will succeed or fail primarily on the strength or weakness of self-effort; the seeker cannot succeed except by relying on God for strength. The student must choose to act; the seeker must choose to allow God to act. The student must want to succeed; the seeker must want God to succeed.

How, then, do structure, commitment, and discipline translate into the quest for union with God? Commitment means we must say yes to the invitation to come to God in love, and to allow the Spirit to begin the work of transformation in us that only God can do. Discipline means that we must persevere in our yes to God by intentionally and continually opening ourselves to God's action in us. Because the process of transformation continues over a lifetime and even into eternity, one yes does not suffice, any more than the "I will" spoken at a marriage ceremony is an assurance of a lifetime of wedded bliss. Our lives must become a continuing yes to God, a continuing effort to respond to God acting in us.

But discipline requires at least some structure to support it. By structure I mean simply a pattern or framework in which we practice our commitment and discipline. The pattern may be very simple—for example, never failing to offer our day to God when we wake up each morning—or it may be as complex as the daily schedule of a monastery, but without a structure we may lack periodic reminders of our commitment. Moreover, without structure we may open ourselves to God only haphazardly, if we remember to do so at all. We must, with some regularity, listen for God's still, small voice. We must, with some regularity, try to discern how God is acting in our lives and how we can then respond most appropriately. Structure provides a regularity in which our discipline can operate more effectively.

Are structure, commitment, and discipline absolutely essential for spiritual progress? God is doing the work, and God works as God will. It is possible for God to take a spiritual beginner and convert that person instantly into someone who belongs wholly, absolutely, and unconditionally to God. But this is not the ordinary path of spiritual progress any more than it is ordinary for a newborn child to be able to recite the Gospels by heart. If God is to do the work, we must allow God the time and the opportunity to do the work. But as helpful as structure, commitment, and discipline can be, there are other aids to spiritual progress that can serve us well, and one of the most helpful is community.

the need for community

Even those who fled urban decadence in the early centuries of the church to live alone in the desert generally found it desirable to form communities for mutual support and to assist one another in facing the spiritual and material rigors of their life. When someone gains a reputation for having extraordinary spiritual gifts, often other seekers gather around that person for guidance and wisdom. Sometimes they form a community around the "master," as happened, for example, with St. Benedict seeking solitude in his cave at Subiaco. The community that is thus brought into being becomes a source of support and strength for its members. They are more of a "family in Christ" than they would have been in isolation. Paul reminds us that we are interdependent as members of the body of Christ. Though there may be those who have achieved deep union with God as "lone rangers," they are the exception rather than the rule. Even in contemplative communities such as the Trappists, a monk is allowed to become a hermit only after proving himself as a member of the community, and the ties to the community are never really broken.

As Christians, we are called to minister to one another. This ministry can be, for example, offering prayer or providing physical or material assistance in time of illness or special need. It can also be providing a compassionate ear when someone needs to talk about his spiritual journey. It can be praying with someone to help discern the voice of the Holy Spirit. It can be just sitting quietly with someone as she wrestles with God in the depths of her soul.

We come together as the people of God to celebrate the liturgy, the "work of the people" of God. And in the Lord's Supper, we are joined with Christ and with one another in a union more intimate than we can understand this side of heaven.

We thus see that having a group of trusted friends with whom we meet on a regular basis, and with whom we share our spiritual journey, can be an immense blessing. Jesus promised that where two or three are gathered in his name, he is there with them. And his sacred presence is no more deeply felt than in such groups where individuals come together to support one another in Christian love.

Being with other pilgrims on the spiritual journey can inspire us to greater devotion and to be more honest and accountable in regard to our own commitment, discipline, and structure. The Holy Spirit is sometimes more clearly heard in the voices of others than in the often confused and distracted thoughts of our own minds.

I often feel humbled and uplifted when I am with other seekers. With them, in them, I sense Christ's presence more fully than when I am alone. I rejoice in their faith and faithfulness. They are an assurance of God's unfailing fidelity to aid us to come to God. They are an expression of God's never failing love. Community can be a powerful spiritual aid. Another powerful spiritual aid in drawing nearer to God is prayer.

the need for prayer

Obviously, one cannot make progress toward a deeper union with God without prayer, because prayer is, by definition, consciously and intentionally pointing ourselves toward God.

We can fail to pray out of laziness—we do not point ourselves toward anything, a sort of nihilism—or we can point ourselves toward that which is not God, which is idolatry. Both of these forms of failure in prayer are more common than we would like to admit, even in those who have a real desire to come to know God. Idolatry, even in denominations that claim to abhor the practice, is relatively common. This idolatry commonly takes the form of creating images of God that we are willing to worship. Although, as human beings, we must think in terms of concepts and images, we may fall into the trap of mistaking our concepts and images of reality for reality itself. Thus, we may assume that our concept of God is God, or at least so similar to God that we are safe in adoring it.

Spiritual development must take as one of its basic premises that we do not know God, and that only through the action of God can we come to such a knowledge. But then we must admit that all of the images of God that we ourselves construct are false because such human-made images cannot hope to capture the fullness of God's infinite character and being. If we cling to the images of God that we have crafted, we will not be able to tell when God begins to reveal himself to us and when we are merely worshiping the god we ourselves have made.*

---

*The topic of images of God provides a good opportunity to address the language used for God in this book. I recognize that God is not a male, and that the use of masculine pronouns to speak of God is off-putting for some people. The dilemma is that alternative methods of expression (feminine pronouns, alternating masculine and feminine pronouns, avoiding pronouns altogether) are equally off-putting for other people. In order to allow myself to concentrate on my subject matter without having to tackle this thorny issue at the same time, I have used masculine pronouns throughout, as is the case in Christian Scripture and in most Christian traditions, but have tried to keep their use to a minimum.

Our prayer, therefore, must include a humble recognition that we stand in error and only God can bring us into the truth.

To embark on a search for God is to embark on a journey as adventurous as that of any secular voyage of discovery, and the rewards are more valuable than any earthly treasure. The tools of the journey include, but are not limited to, commitment, structure, discipline, community, and prayer.

If we want to create a close-knit community of seekers for mutual support and prayer on the journey, how might we go about this, and what would such a group look like?

CREATING A SPIRITUAL DEVELOPMENT GROUP

THE FOLLOWING RECOMMENDATIONS ARE SUGGESTIONS ONLY. The advice I offer here is gleaned from working with spiritual development groups over a number of years, but different circumstances and temperaments may call for different guidelines. Follow my advice if it seems reasonable and helpful in setting up your group, but always be open to the inspiration of the Holy Spirit and the needs of the group.

A spiritual development group should generally have no more than ten to twelve members. A group that is too large may intimidate the shyer members and will give less time for each member to share. On the other hand, a group that is too small, say only three or four, may not produce the helpful diversity and range of insights of a larger group.

The members of the group need not share the same theological views or be members of the same church, but they should be willing to listen with patience and compassion to whatever other members of the group may say. A spiritual development group is not primarily a study group. It is a gathering of pilgrims on a journey. All members should honor and love one another in Christ Jesus.

Members must feel safe in sharing their personal stories and beliefs, or they will withhold them. A person who feels criticized or judged either will quickly leave the group or will stay but share only what he or she believes the group wants to hear. The group will no longer be useful to that member, and likely to others as well, because spiritual development implies a willingness to respect the integrity of others, even when we disagree with their opinions.

We need to remind ourselves frequently that it is God who is doing the real work, and the members of the group are but instruments to help each other gain greater insights into God's action in their individual lives. A member who presumes to step into the place of God risks not only presumption, but stifling the action of the Spirit as well.

Some members by nature, or perhaps initially from fear of ridicule, may be reluctant to voice their opinions or reveal their true feelings and experiences concerning spiritual matters. All members should be encouraged to speak, because mutual sharing is an important part of building trust and providing mutual support. But no one should be forced to speak to share anything unwillingly. Nor should the group be afraid of silence. If no one has anything to say, no harm will be done if the group prays silently or quietly reflects on the issues before it.

Those who join the group should be committed to both the group and the process adopted by the group. This means that attendance should be one of each member's highest priorities. There are, of course, numerous valid reasons to miss a meeting, but frequent absences may interfere with creating a sense of community, and may also hinder the continuity of discussions and study since the absent members must be brought up to speed later on, and they may repeat questions and subject matter already covered during their absence.

Any member who must be absent on a specific date would do well to notify the convener for that date. If several members will be absent on that date, the meeting might be canceled or rescheduled for a more amenable time.

I recommend that the meetings take place at a church to avoid placing a burden on a host, and to emphasize that the meeting is not primarily a social occasion. The chance of distractions is diminished if the group meets in a quiet room apart from other functions that might be taking place at the same time. But I stress again that each group must set its own ground rules and, in many situations, a private home may be the location in which the group can best function.

Interruptions, however, should be kept to a minimum. Some groups take the phone off the hook or let the answering machine pick up all calls. If a member is expecting an urgent call, that fact might be made known to the group in advance so that the member's response to a call is understood and excused as an unusual circumstance. Efforts should be made to help the group focus as best it can on the issues before it and to avoid needless distractions. For example, a group may decide to forgo refreshments if these would impose an undue burden on some member, or if the group felt that refreshments would be a distraction.

The group is not an end in itself. It is a spiritual aid and a means to support each member in his or her progress toward union with God. Whatever style the group adopts, the group must keep its reason for being squarely in view.

the content and format of the sessions

The principal purpose of the sessions in Part Two is to assist group members in developing an intentional theological and structural foundation for spiritual growth. These sessions lead toward the development of a "rule of life" and a basic understanding of spiritual direction. The group is then asked to consider if it wants to continue to meet to provide group spiritual direction for its members. Suggestions for how the group might engage in group spiritual direction are provided in Part Three.

Each session (except the first) begins with a "Sharing of Experiences and Insights." The group is free to address whichever of the questions proposed it wishes, or even to devise additional questions, but the purpose of this exercise is to provide a measure of accountability in regard to the homework assignments and to allow members to share their special spiritual ideas and experiences. They may also discuss how well or poorly the program is impacting their lives.

A session continues with a brief review of a few keys points from previous sessions, particularly those that should be kept in mind while reading the study material in the current session. Then follows a brief overview of the purpose of the session.

The "Material for Study and Discussion" is the heart of the session. Each presentation tries to provide information that a participant can apply in strengthening his or her spiritual life. Members are encouraged to read this section prior to the group meeting at which it will be discussed, but it would probably be best if the group were to read it again in its entirety at the meeting before discussion to insure that the section is fresh in members' minds.

Following the material for discussion are "Review Questions" to test the group's basic understanding of the notions presented. Then follow "Additional Questions for Discussion." The group should probably stick with the review questions until all members feel they can comfortably answer them, but how many of the additional questions are considered is up to the group.

Finally, a "Homework Assignment" is given. The homework is an integral part of the program and essential to getting the most benefit from it.

The group is free to proceed at its own pace. Although the material is arranged by sessions, a session does not have to be completed in one meeting. How much can or should be covered will be determined by a number of factors, including how long the meeting is scheduled to last and whether the discussion of some question or idea is so productive that it should be allowed to run on beyond the scheduled time.

Once a group has been formed to consider this material, how might its meetings be organized?

the structure of meetings that address the material in this book

While the suggestions concerning small groups given earlier might be applicable to any small group whose members wish to share life experiences and provide mutual support, the suggestions now are more specifically directed toward the small groups for whom this book was written. Although the group may choose to apply the guidelines proposed below to get started, the group is always free to adopt such procedures as it finds will help make the members more comfortable and the process more fruitful. Nevertheless, members should have a common understanding of how the group will function so that the group can better stay the course and avoid unnecessary conflict or embarrassment.

A group, once formed, should agree on how frequently to meet—for example, twice a month, on the first and third Mondays at 7:30 P.M. Whatever arrangement best suits the members is fine, but meetings should generally be spaced at least two weeks apart to allow members time to reflect on the readings and practice the exercises. My own experience has been that ninety minutes are needed to cover the material properly and allow for discussion and prayer.

A convener should be designated for each meeting, though the role of convener may well rotate through the group. The convener is not to rule the group, but rather, to make sure that all things take place in good order. If there is someone in the group who is an experienced spiritual director, the group might allow that individual to exercise the role of a mentor, but as a rule, all members of the group should be on an equal footing. Allowing a small number of individuals to dominate the conversation or, worse, to manipulate or intimidate other members, is one of the best means to insure that the group will have a short life and little positive effect.

When the meeting is to begin, the convener calls the group to order. The first order of business may be several minutes of silence to give members a chance to collect themselves, recognize God's presence, and dedicate themselves to what is to take place at that meeting, that is, opening oneself to the transforming love of God.

A good way for members of a group to become better acquainted at the outset is to share spiritual autobiographies; thus, the members begin to appreciate one another's stories and value how God brought each of them to where they are now. These spiritual autobiographies do not have to be exhaustive (that can make them exhausting), but they might highlight some of the "God moments" of a member's life and give insights into how God kindled the desire for spiritual growth that brought the member to the group.

Whatever rules the group decides to operate by, these should be decided before beginning the material, although the rules may be amended later.

Members are likely to obtain the most benefit from the material if they read and think about a session prior to the meeting at which that session will be considered. It may also prove useful to read the reflection again out loud before discussing it to refresh members' memories of its content and to make sure that all members present know what is to be discussed.

The convener is responsible for keeping people focused on relevant material, although the Spirit should be given room to "breathe as it will." To help members stay on track and to have something to share, I encourage them to write down a brief summary of any experience or insight that they might bring to the group as soon as possible after having it.

The convener should remember that the purpose of the group

is not to resolve the problems of the church, or to allow members to air their personal problems. Sometimes, however, a member may experience a major crisis, such as the death of a loved one or a serious illness, and need the support and prayers of the group. Reasonable and compassionate allowance should be made for this contingency.

Each member should be encouraged, but never pressured, to share his or her views. There should be no negative criticism of any opinion expressed, although persons may state that they disagree with a speaker if their tone in so doing is neither condescending nor judgmental. Rarely will there be closure on answers, and closure should not be expected. When the meeting is to end, the convener announces the time and place of the next meeting and closes the session with a prayer.

PART TWO

SESSION 1
where's this bus headed and who's driving?

BEFORE STARTING THE FIRST SESSION, LET'S LOOK AT SOME RE-minders concerning procedure:

1. The group is free to proceed at its own pace. Although the material is arranged by sessions, a session does not have to be completed in one meeting. How much can or should be covered will be determined by a number of factors, including how long the meeting is to last and whether the discussion of some question or idea is so productive that it should be allowed to run on.

2. Not all of the questions in "Sharing of Experiences and Insights" and "Additional Questions for Discussion" need to be addressed. The group or the convener can select those that are most appealing or relevant.

3. The "Material for Study and Discussion" should general-ly be read at the meeting at which it is to be considered. This will insure that all members of the group have read it at least once, and that it is fresh in everyone's memory.

4. The group might wish to begin each meeting with a short period of silence to give members an opportunity to focus their attention before an opening prayer. This may help bring members "into the room" and lessen distracting side conversations or diversions from whatever the group is to consider at that meeting.

5. Members are encouraged to keep a journal between meetings on their spiritual insights, questions, and experiences, as well as on their reflections on the reading or assignments, for sharing at the next meeting, and also to take notes during meetings on any points they find especially helpful so that they can review them later.

introduction: a review of the group's rules
The convener should review the rules under which the group has decided to operate. This reminds the members of the framework within which the group will function and provides an opportunity to clarify ambiguities or to make modest adjustments. Since the group has previously had a chance to discuss its rules, the convener should steer the group away from significant redrafting. The group is always free to revise or add to its rules later as experience dictates.

purpose of the first session
This session reflects upon the destiny to which we are called as Christians and our complete dependence on God's help in achieving that destiny.

material for study and discussion
Paul tells us that we are called to see God "face to face," to know God as God as knows us. We are destined to do more than learn about God; we are to come to an intimate knowledge of God.

We would never have dared ask for such a gift unless God had promised to give it to us freely. Indeed, we would never have even known that such a gift is possible if God had not revealed it to us through our Lord, Jesus Christ. Just as Jesus and God are one—that is, Jesus' human nature is intimately and indivisibly bound to his divine nature—so too we, through our union with Christ, can come into union with God, and through this union come to "see" God directly.

I place "see" in quotation marks because the manner in which we will see God cannot be through our ordinary means of sight. Our knowledge of the world around us comes through the senses. Our sensory data is processed by our mental faculties. For example, we abstract from all the chairs we see to create in our minds the concept "chair," so that when we encounter an object we have never encountered before, we can decide if it is a chair. Skilled artisans can create new designs for chairs that are both attractive and comfortable, or an author might write a short story about the role a chair played in an old man's life; thus, we can combine concepts and ideas originally gained from the senses to create new concepts and ideas.

But everything we can know using all of our natural powers is not God. God totally and absolutely lies beyond the reach of our senses and our unaided mental abilities. The problem is not that we are not smart enough or that we have not studied enough. Rather, God lies completely outside the realm of the natural abilities of even the most brilliant scholar who ever lived. Great theologians may know a lot about God, but even they cannot know God directly except through divine power and grace working in them.

We cannot confine the infinite God in any concepts or images or notions that can be contained in our finite minds. We cannot know God without divine intervention to give us that knowledge. Only God can give us knowledge of God.

Here, then, are some facts of which we should be convinced related to our knowledge of God and of ourselves:

1. We cannot know God except by divine gift and intervention, even though we can, through Scripture and other forms of prayer and study, learn a great deal about God.

2. Since we can fully know ourselves only by knowing how

God sees us, and this knowledge of ourselves comes only from knowing God, we cannot even truly know ourselves without divine intervention.

3. Because of Jesus Christ and his reconciling work, we can be certain that, if we ask, we will be given the gifts we need to know God perfectly.

4. If we want God to act in our lives to bring us to the knowledge of him, we must provide opportunities for such action. God will not act without our consent.

In other words, without the light of God we are in darkness about ourselves and about God. We cannot even recognize our helplessness, our sinfulness, our fallibility and vulnerability—which should be starkly apparent—unless we somehow are given to understand the power and the goodness of God.

But God is supremely One. We cannot divide God into parts or distinguish between God's being and attributes. In human beings we can make these distinctions. I can distinguish Sally's ability to play the piano from the color of her hair. I can distinguish Sam's nose from his arm. Although such distinctions are real with regard to objects we can know through our senses, and although mentally we are able to apply different adjectives, like "good" and "merciful," to God, there are no such distinctions found in God's being per se. Goodness and mercy are characteristics of God, but we cannot separate God's goodness and mercy from God's being. God is supremely One and cannot be divided into parts. Therefore we can know the power and the goodness of God only by knowing God.

God, however, cannot be known by our human intellect, and cannot be confined in or limited by our ideas. We cannot describe God with words, nor can we paint a picture that shows us what God looks like. God can only be known by the experience of him, an experience that only the Spirit can give us. In that experience we recognize our inadequacy and utter dependence on God alone.

If we are totally dependent on God to come to know God, then what hope is there? Are we not doomed to remain forever separated from the knowledge of God? But we need not despair. Through Jesus Christ we have the promise that we will be granted the knowledge (experience) of God if we truly want it. God leaves the critical first step to us, which is, in truth, the only step we are capable of making: to choose to want to know God, to accept the invitation to come to know God intimately, just as God knows us.

But choosing to want to know God involves not merely asking for the experience of God, or just saying yes to God's invitation, because this divine experience is life-transforming. To wish to participate in the experience (life) of God is more radical than choosing a mate or selecting a particular vocation in life. The experience of God will involve an emptying out of ourselves, a recognition that we are literally nothing and God is everything. It is declaring to God, "I truly want to love you with all my heart and soul and mind and strength." Only in the experience of God will we come to recognize the full implication of our choice.

Nevertheless, if we say that we want God to take possession of our lives, but we leave no opportunity for that to happen, then we are frustrating God's intention and saying by our actions that we are not serious about what we declare with our words. We must open our hearts and minds to the action of God.

review questions

1. What is our destiny as Christians?

2. Can we achieve this destiny through our own efforts?

3. If we cannot achieve this destiny through our own efforts, then how can this destiny be achieved?

4. What must we do ourselves if we are to achieve this destiny as Christians?

additional questions for discussion

1. Suppose that through my own efforts alone—perhaps by carefully studying Scripture or by saying certain words over and over again—I could come to a direct knowledge of God. What would this say about God? What would this say about Christianity?

2. Can you share any experiences that convinced you of your complete dependence on God to come to God?

3. Can you describe an important "God moment" in your life thus far?

4. Some religions and philosophies say that a human being can achieve a knowledge of God, or even become God or a god, by performing certain exercises or acquiring secret knowledge without any outside help. Why might such a belief appeal to someone? What problems do you see with it?

5. God is a mystery in the sense that God cannot be understood by using our natural mental powers no matter how long or hard we study. What other mysteries were mentioned in the reading? Are you concerned that many truths of our faith are mysteries? Does the fact that we are dealing with mysteries create problems with describing our faith to others? How do you address this problem?

homework assignment:
an exercise on the quiet presence of god

One way that we provide opportunities for God to transform us and demonstrate that we have made a choice for God is by adopting and being faithful to a "rule of life." (We develop the concept of a rule of life in sessions 9 and 10.) A rule of life usually contains elements of prayer, study, and action. Today, we begin to look at prayer.

Prayer essentially consists of directing our minds and our

actions to God. If we offer all that we do to God, then we can pray always. Even our sleep can be prayer if we offer it to the Lord so we can refresh ourselves for divine service.

But the specific form of prayer that we choose to make part of our rule of life should be some form of prayer that opens our minds more fully to the action of God; that is, it makes us more available to God, not just by our speaking to God, but by leaving room for God to communicate with us.

Ordinarily, our minds are filled with distractions. When we try to be silent, many thoughts still pass through our minds. Many households have a radio or television going even though no one is paying attention to it. If we are to become adept at prayer, we must become comfortable with silence. (See the account of Elijah on Mount Horeb in 1 Kings 19; God was not in the whirlwind or the fire or the earthquake, but in the still, small voice.) We must practice the art of solitude, even in the middle of noise, if necessary.

The assignment to carry out at home is to practice the silent presence of God for no less than five minutes each day. Here's how to do this. Find a place of silence. Get comfortable and close your eyes. Direct your mind toward God. Tell God, "I want to love you with all my heart and soul and mind and strength." Tell God, "Take possession of my life and make it your own." Imagine lifting yourself up as an offering to God. Then, as best you can, simply remain silent in the presence of God.

SESSION 2
what's the problem with sin?

sharing of experiences and insights

The practice of the silent presence of God was introduced as the homework assignment in session 1. In that exercise we remind ourselves that God is always present with us and then allow ourselves to rest comfortably and quietly in that presence. Though every human being has internal distractions that they cannot control, we can best carry out this exercise in a posture and setting in which we reduce outside distractions to a minimum. Here are questions for group sharing based on the assignment:

1. Were you able to do this exercise? If not, what obstacles prevented you? How might these obstacles be circumvented in the future?

2. The harder you fight distractions, the more powerful they become. Were you able to let distractions go by without paying any attention to them, just as you might ignore traffic noise outside a window? Were you able to find any other strategies to prevent distractions from interfering with your silent companionship with God?

3. Did you receive any special insights during this prayer time? Do you have any other spiritual insights or experiences since the last session that you wish to share?

review of some key points from the previous session

We are invited by God to share in the life of God; eventually, we are to know God as God knows us, to see God face to face. But we of ourselves do not have the power to bring this about. It can happen only through divine power acting in us. We must say yes to God's invitation and open ourselves to the transformation that the Spirit will bring about in us if we allow it to happen.

purpose of the second session

In the second session we reflect on the nature of sin as any obstacle that interferes with the divine grace that transforms us into what God wants us to become.

material for study and discussion

What we believe about God and how we define our relation to God deeply colors our concept of sin. If we believe that God is a vengeful judge and we are criminals before the bench, then sin becomes a test of our obedience. Sin is defined by what God orders us to do or to avoid doing, under pain of punishment if we disobey. God, however, does not need obedience to feed his ego or prove his potency. Moreover, viewing sin in terms of crime and punishment may hinder spiritual growth because God is envisioned as someone to be feared rather than loved, someone unapproachable rather than someone with whom we are to become intimate. Carried to its extreme, the image of an angry avenger can drive people away from God, since the devil himself may seem less threatening and terrible.

Some say that if someone does not sin out of fear of punishment, then he or she will eventually be led to seek God out of love. Although this may be true, it is not appropriate that those who love God should be afraid of God. In his first epistle St. John tells us, "Perfect love casts out fear."

If we believe that God is a friend, then sin is an offense against a friend. We try to avoid sin in order to please and remain on good terms with God. Implicit in this attitude, however, may be the view that God will favor us with friendship and reward us if we avoid sin, but will withdraw friendship if we do sin. We may still think that God has ordered us to obey certain rules to test whether we are really his friends. Thus, we must earn God's friendship by obedience to these rules. Obedience to the will of God out of hope of reward is self-interest rather than unconditional love.

We recall from the first session that we do not yet know God, nor do we yet know ourselves, since we can only know ourselves if we see ourselves as God sees us. God's will is to allow us to share in the divine nature so that we can see him face to face. We are to experience God as God experiences himself and know ourselves as God knows us. What sin is must somehow be related to the goal that sin hinders us from achieving.

We will define sin as any obstacle that hinders God from achieving work in us to draw us more deeply into union with him. Of course, setting our own wills deliberately against the will of God—sin in the traditional sense—is sin in this extended sense as well.

If God commands us to live in a particular way, he does so out of love, since if we live as God intends us to live, the Spirit is better able to act in our lives and work in and through us to bring about the Kingdom in us and through us. Without our cooperation and consent, God cannot bring us to himself. God offers, but we must accept. If we choose to go our own way, even to the loneliness of hell, God allows us our choice. God does not so much judge as make us choose.

Remember that it is only through God that we can come to God. (We will discuss the need for Christ later on, since it is through Christ that we have hope of union with God.) We, however, must choose to allow God to transform us; that is, we must throw open our hearts to God, make ourselves available to him, show by our choices that we truly want the Spirit to take possession of our lives and teach us to love God. Whenever we deliberately choose against God, we are saying to God that we are not really serious about wanting God more than anything else, that we prefer our own will to the divine will, that we are willing to settle for less than what he offers us, which is himself. (This does not mean that we will never sin, but, even when we do sin, we can renew our choice for God and ask for forgiveness, which is always granted if we sincerely repent.)

But we may have sins in the broader sense described above of which we ourselves are unaware, obstacles we do not even know about, sins known only to God. If we are to come to love God with all our heart and soul and mind and strength, then whatever portions of our heart or soul or mind or strength that do not yet belong entirely to God are obstacles to perfect love; they are sins in the sense in which we have defined sin in this session. God alone can bring us to perfect love, removing those obstacles through divine power that we cannot remove by ourselves, even if we recognized them. Just as we have expanded the notion of sin, we may expand the notion of forgiveness by defining it to be this purifying power of God that can bring us to the deepest love of which creatures are capable.

Our Christian life should be a love story: learning to love as we have first been loved, being brought into union with the object of our love. As we come to know the love of God (which is God himself), we will come to know the imperfection of our own love, our sinfulness, our own nothingness in the face of the One who is All. This, however, should not bring despair but hope, because we can firmly rely on God to fulfill the promise to bring us to himself.

review questions

1. What is sin as defined in this session?

2. How does this definition of sin differ from the notion of sin as willful disobedience of God's commands?

3. Are we capable of ridding our lives of all sin? What should we do if we do consciously sin?

additional questions for discussion

1. If you were God, how would you treat someone who deliberately disobeyed you? If you are or were a parent, how do or would you treat a child who deliberately disobeyed you? Are your two responses consistent with one another?

2. Are there sins—that is, obstacles to union with God—so great that they cannot be overcome? If so, describe such a sin. If not, why not?

3. What do you think is the primary obstacle to God's transforming grace in us; that is, what is the most common sin?

4. If God had chosen to do so, could God have created us so that we could not sin? If God had done so, would we also have had free will and the ability to love?

homework assignment: discipline and mortification

If we are to choose consistently for God, then we must, with divine help, strengthen our wills. We might therefore "exercise" our will by making choices that are contrary to our natural inclinations. These small acts of mortification (self-denial), or discipline of the will, should be carried out secretly and with the intention of offering them to God as signs of our love, that is, signs or symbolic acts to show that we choose God above all else and are willing to give up anything to be his alone. We can also lift up these acts as prayers that God will teach us how to love him.

Consciously select some way in which you can discipline your will and offer yourself to God through some of your choices. This may involve an extra act of kindness, or passing up a snack, or not taking a smoke when you feel the urge. The choices are yours, but they should be secrets between you and God, little acts of love offered freely to the beloved and not to please yourself or someone else, much less to make anyone else think more highly of you.

Each time you do an act of self-denial, consciously tell God, "I am willing to give up whatever is necessary to love you as you have first loved me." Offer your will to God, asking that your will be conformed to his.

If you found the exercise on the quiet presence of God useful (introduced as an assignment in session 1), you might wish to continue that as well.

SESSION 3
holy—who, me?

sharing of experiences and insights

1. The assignment given at the last meeting was to offer God occasional small acts of self-denial or mortification. The word "mortification" comes from Latin words meaning "to make dead." We are to die to self so that we might live more fully in God. We were to offer these acts to God in love, saying that we choose him above all else and would be willing to give up all else if we could have him alone. We were also to ask God to teach us how to love him. Did you carry out this exercise? If not, what obstacles prevented you? What steps did you take to try to overcome them?

2. How do you feel about turning more control of your life over to God? What would it mean to give up all else to have God alone? Does this mean that God wants us to abandon our families and jobs? If our wills are more closely aligned with God's will, will we love our family less? How will our love of our family change as we love God more?

3. Does anyone have any special spiritual experiences or insights to share with the group?

review of some key points from previous sessions

Our goal is to come to the direct knowledge of God by allowing God to transform us by divine power to bring us to that knowledge. Because God alone can bring us to such knowledge, we must open ourselves so that God can do this work for us. Sin is anything that is an obstacle to God's transforming grace in us.

purpose of the third session

As members of Christ's body, we are consecrated to God, a holy people, called to be perfect, even as our heavenly Father is perfect. This session explores the notions of consecration, holiness, and perfection.

material for study and discussion

Consecration involves setting something apart for God. Generally, something or someone is consecrated, set apart for God, by some ritual. In the Old Testament, an animal was sacrificed (the word "sacrifice" comes from Latin words meaning "to make sacred"). By ritually slaughtering the animal, a Jewish priest consecrated that animal to God.

A human being is set apart for God not by a literal death but by a symbolic dying with Christ in going down into the waters of baptism (which represent the tomb) and rising a new person in Christ as he or she comes forth from the saving water. The bread and the wine are consecrated in the Communion celebration to become the body and blood of Christ. A pastor is consecrated to be a shepherd to the people and a source of the sacramental life of the church. Persons taking vows in religious orders are said to be consecrating their lives to God, setting their lives apart in a special way for God.

Consecration takes place only by the power of God. Through special services, many denominations ask God to bless a building for use as a church. In ordinations, we ask God to set apart, or consecrate, someone for ministry. Even the special consecration of religious vows makes sense only in the context of a special call from God to the religious life, and God provides grace for the person under vows to be faithful to his or her sacred promises.

But all Christians are truly consecrated. They are set apart for God in many ways. First, in baptism, Christians have been made members of the body of Christ as well as children of God and heirs of heaven. In baptism, Christians have passed from the slavery of sin into the freedom of the sons and daughters of God. They have mystically died with Christ and risen with him from the grave. The life of the baptized person no longer belongs to him or her, but to God.

Second, Christians, and even more broadly, all human beings, are a purchased people, ransomed by the blood of Christ. Humans stand in a new relationship with the Father because of the incarnation. It is not even so much that Christ died for us (although he did) as that God united the divine nature with a human nature. No longer is humanity separated from its Creator. A closer bond now exists between God and humanity than existed when Adam and Eve walked in Paradise before the fall. Adam and Eve's relationship with God was that of creatures with their Creator, but Scripture does not declare that Adam and Eve were intimately bonded with God, nor is there any reason to suggest that they did, or could come to, know God as God knows himself, however happy they may have been in a natural sense. Whatever virtues Adam and Eve may have had before the fall, no one suggests that they had any hope of ascending through God's transforming power into the very life of the God who created them.

But Christians do have this hope, because God has promised that this is possible through the Incarnate Word, Jesus Christ. Just as Christ is one with the Father, we are to be one with Christ, and through him to be one with the Father as well. He is the way to the Father. He is the life of God. He is the truth, that is, the knowledge of the ultimate reality, which is none other than God.

St. Gregory the Great once said, "Christian, know thy dignity!" This dignity too many Christians forget or make light of. Many would be quite content to walk again in the Garden of Paradise as did Adam and Eve, or stroll golden streets, as some imagine heaven to contain. But Christians have an even higher calling. They are consecrated, set apart for God alone, destined to be transformed by the power of the Holy Spirit into nothing less than God. As Athanasius said, "God became man so that man might become God." And we dare to proclaim this because Christ himself proclaimed it. Just as he did not lose his human nature in his divine nature, but the two were each complete but inseparable from one another, we too are called, while retaining our human nature, to "become by grace what God is by nature." And how is this to come about? It is through our being joined to Christ and through our being transformed by the power of the Holy Spirit. We are members of Christ and temples of the Holy Spirit.

We must recognize that our lives are consecrated. Once we recognize what this means, it will color all our actions, for all we do is done in the realization that we are God's and God is ours.

Because we are consecrated, we are also holy. Whatever belongs to God is necessarily holy. But every human being is all too well aware that there is much that belongs to him or her that does not yet fully belong to God. One person has a desire for power that interferes with his relationship with God and causes him to act contrary to what he knows to be God's will for him. Another person unduly wants others to think well of her, and so she agrees with what someone says even though she knows that it is untrue or unfairly hurtful of others.

This is nothing more than saying that every human being still has obstacles to union with God—every human being is sinful.

We must cooperate with God so that the Spirit can make us "whole," that is, completely God's.

This is what Christ meant when he told us to be perfect as our heavenly Father is perfect. We are to imitate Christ's perfection. Why was Christ perfect? It was not because he had the perfect height, or the perfect color eyes, or because of any physical attribute. Christ was perfect because his human will was always in total harmony with his divine will. He always did the will of his Father. Every action of Christ, every choice he made, was made in accordance with the will of God.

We must strive for the same perfection that Christ had; that is, we must try as best we can to conform our wills to God's will for us. If our wills are perfectly in tune with God's will, it doesn't matter what prayer techniques we use or what emotions we feel during prayer. We are perfect to the degree that we choose what we believe God wants us to choose. Indeed, as God brings us into more perfect union with himself, our whole life becomes a prayer. Our whole life is directed to God in love.

review questions

1. What does it mean for something to be consecrated?

2. How have we as Christians been consecrated?

3. What does it mean for something to be holy?

4. How are we called to be perfect as Christ and our heavenly Father are perfect?

5. Is it necessary to feel emotionally that we are consecrated in order to *be* consecrated? To be holy? To have our will in harmony with God's will?

additional questions for discussion

1. Can you give additional examples of rituals by which something or someone is consecrated?

2. Is consecration unique to Judaism and Christianity? What other religious groups might honor some rite of consecration?

3. Even if we study the Scriptures and pray for guidance, we cannot always be sure what God wants us to do in every situation. With which of our choices do you believe God is most concerned? Do you believe that God "micromanages"?

4. Thomas Merton, a noted Roman Catholic monastic and writer, said that he did not know if what he did pleased God, but he was sure that his desire to please God pleased God. Do you agree with this statement? If we are not sure what choice God wants us to make in a particular situation, how should we act? Should we refuse to act until we are certain of God's will?

homework assignment: praying the psalms

We now explore another prayer technique: praying the psalms. Are you angry with God? Read Psalms 22 and 55. Do you want to praise God? Read Psalms 138 and 147. There is truly a psalm for every mood and occasion. Don't be afraid to speak your heart to God, whatever your concerns and feelings may be. The psalmist has already said as much and more.

Instead of reading an entire psalm, you might choose just one or two verses that you find especially appropriate for your current mood and situation and read them over several times. Each time use a different inflection. Think about what you are reading. Identify with the author of the psalm and imagine how he might have felt. Direct your thoughts to God in the spirit of the psalm.

Spend some time each day praying the psalms. This can replace your practice of the quiet presence of God, or you may choose to continue that exercise and add this new exercise.

SESSION 4
that wondrous cross

sharing of experiences and insights

1. Did you find praying the psalms helpful? What feelings did you experience in this exercise?

2. How did praying the psalms differ for you from practicing the quiet presence of God? Was this difference(s) positive or negative, and why?

3. Do you find it difficult to tell God that you are angry with him? Do you think it is always sinful to be angry, particularly with God? What emotions have you felt toward God in the last month? How (if at all) did you express these emotions? How did you feel in the wake of such expression (or nonexpression)?

4. Do you have any special insights to share?

5. Of the various exercises proposed thus far (in sessions 1-3), which have you found the most useful in your personal spiritual journey and why?

review of some key points from previous sessions

Because of our membership in the body of Christ, we are consecrated to God. We belong to God and therefore are holy because God is holy. But we are also called to be perfect, that is, to conform our wills to the divine will so that the Spirit can draw us more completely into God's own life.

purpose of the fourth session

In this session we reflect on Christ's death on the cross and the lessons that this holds for us as we try to open ourselves to God's transforming grace.

material for study and discussion

The early church viewed the sacrifice of Christ on the cross primarily in the light of the Mosaic law. Under that law, animals were ritually slain to atone—that is, to offer ransom or payment to God—for the sins of human beings. It was, of course, the human sinners who deserved to be punished, but the law stated that animals could substitute for the sinner, and, through the sacrifice of the animals, God forgave the sinner.

The atonement under the Old Testament was substitutionary. The animal died as a substitute for the sinner. But the sacrifices had to be repeated continually, since the substitution was imperfect. No sacrifice was sufficient in itself to "pay" for the sins of the people.

With Christ's sacrifice on the cross, a perfect sacrifice was made, a sacrifice of infinite value that of itself could ransom humanity from all of its sins forever. With the atoning sacrifice of the cross, the animal sacrifices of the Old Testament were no longer necessary.

Thus, one view of Christ's death on the cross is that Christ thereby made complete satisfaction for our sins. According to this view, our sins are offenses against God, crimes that demand satisfaction. Because God is infinite in dignity, the satisfaction sin demands must also be infinite. Consequently, only the sacrifice of an infinite being can measure up to what is demanded in order to pay our debt to God. Christ's death was the infinite sacrifice that paid the debt for all of our sins for all time.

But this explanation of Christ's death on the cross, though theologically sound, may mislead us. It implies that Christ *had* to die a shameful death so that God could be appeased. Rather than providing us with an image of a God of love, it provides an image of an angry, vengeful God. Moreover because Christ, as the Incarnate Word, was infinite in dignity, *any* satisfaction he might have made on our behalf with the Father would have had infinite dignity and would have sufficed to make reparation for our offenses. For example, the discomfort that Christ suffered in his birth would have been adequate. The death on the cross was "overkill" from the narrow viewpoint of satisfying an "angry God" who demanded recompense for the indignity he suffered because of human disobedience.

The narrow view of the atonement on the cross remains tied too closely to the Old Testament relationship between God and the people of God, a servant/master relationship rather than a parent/child relationship. It also portrays God in the role of an autocrat hungry for blood to avenge his wounded pride. This is not an attractive image of God. Rather, it is an image of God that often drives potential converts away from Christ and his loving Father, rather than drawing humanity into the arms of a genuinely loving and merciful God. Even in the Old Testament, God tells the people that he is far less interested in burnt offerings and blood sacrifices than in justice and mercy. God would rather be worshiped in spirit and in truth than through ritual offerings that bring no change of heart.

Recall that sin as we defined it in session 2 is any obstacle that interferes with God's efforts to draw us more deeply into his own life. The most serious sin, of course, is deliberate sin, where we knowingly and willingly choose against what we believe to be the will of God; but still, we can thwart God's action within us simply out of ignorance. Without direct divine intervention, we cannot achieve the experience of God or even have any hope for union with God. Without direct divine intervention, our "original sin," our natural inability to come into union with God because we are only creatures, is complete.

But in Christ we find the means to conquer sin. Through Christ the obstacles to union with God can be overcome. The incarnation tells us that Christ is both fully human and fully divine. Through our union with Christ, who unites within himself both divine and human natures, we can, in turn, find union with God.

If Christ had been just a human being and not God, then he could not be the means for us to share in the life of God any more than any other created being can give us this ability. And if Christ had only been God and not a human being, he also could not be the means for us to share in the life of God, because he would not be a bridge between created being (us) and uncreated being (God). The Incarnation is our principal path to God through Christ, who is the way, the truth, and the life. It is the Incarnation that is central to our being able to share in the life of God.

But, then, what role does the cross play? The primary message of the cross is not that an angry Father demands a blood sacrifice of his Son in order to be appeased. Such a view smacks too much of pagans throwing a maiden into the volcano to pacify the volcano god and prevent an eruption. Stressing this concilliatory aspect of the cross is an obstacle to evangelism and to spiritual growth. There are, however, numerous positive and instructive messages we can draw from the cross. Here are some of them:

> God is willing to go to any length to bring us to himself. God is even willing to suffer death, as it were, so that we might gain new life. The cross is not a symbol of the anger of God toward sin but of the love of God for sinful humanity.

> In choosing God above all else, we should expect to suffer. In following Christ, we should not expect to avoid

suffering any more than he sought to avoid it. Indeed, Calvary is a necessary stop along the path to Easter. By choosing God over the world, the world may treat us as it treated Christ. Moreover, Christ's death on the cross is a foreshadowing of our death to ourselves as we are drawn more deeply into the life of God. There is no easy, painless path to union with God, and anyone who promises such a path is a false teacher.

❧ Christ has given us an example of absolute, unconditional love, love that we must imitate if we are to be like him. Christ commanded us to love others as we have first been loved. The love we have received is a sacrificial love, willing to give up everything, even life itself, to bring others to God. If the only way that our worst enemy could come to God was by our dying, then we should be willing to die to bring that person into the Kingdom. That is how we have first been loved.

❧ Our sins can cause intense pain in others. Our sins made the sacrifice of the cross necessary, not so much to appease God as to show us the gravity of choosing our own will over the will of God.

When we love people, we want to share their joys and sorrows and be there with them in times of trouble. Christ still hangs on the cross through the suffering members of his body. He still reaches out in love to many who turn their backs on him. Can we believe that Christ and his saints do not suffer, even though many members of Christ's body still suffer and many more people remain to be converted? If we ourselves grieve when our own children experience pain, can Christ then ignore the pain of his brothers and sisters here on earth? Beware, because to share in the life of Christ is to share in his suffering as well as his peace and his joy.

review questions

1. What is meant by the Incarnation?

2. Why is the Incarnation important to our being able to grow into the life of God?

3. What are four basic lessons we can learn from Christ's death on the cross?

4. Should we expect a pain-free progress as the Spirit draws us into the life of God? Why or why not?

additional questions for discussion

1. Have you ever experienced pain or loss because you acted as your conscience dictated?

2. Which lesson of the cross is most attractive to you? Why?

3. Christ's love was unconditional and unselfish. He wanted to bring every human being into the Kingdom, and he had no thought of personal reward in doing so. Is human love usually this way? Is our love of God unconditional and unselfish? Would we love God as much if we did not want the reward of heaven or if we did not fear the punishment of hell? Do we really want to share the joys of heaven with our worst enemies?

homework assignment: study

Although we cannot come to know or experience God through study, God wants us to develop our minds so that the Spirit can better use us in his service. Moreover, spiritual study is itself a form of prayer that points the mind toward God. The discipline of study also underlines our commitment to open our minds and hearts to God. While we pray for God to mold us, we do not sit idle but open ourselves to the divine Word, wherever it might be found—in holy scriptures, in thoughtful literature, in creation, in the wise counsel of a friend, family member, or stranger on the street.

Pick a book—the Bible is fine, but you may wish to do reading in some particular area, such as healing or prayer—and decide on a specific study goal for each day. Be realistic; perhaps one chapter of the Bible or a few pages of another work is all you have time for, particularly if you are going to continue other exercises as well. Read whatever you read with an open heart and mind. If you come across a passage that calls to you, stop and think about it rather than pushing on. Study is not just a means of learning, but an opportunity to listen to what God might be trying to teach you. Particularly consider how you can apply what you are learning to shape your own life more in accordance with God's will for you.

SESSION 5
growing up spiritually

sharing of experiences and insights

1. What did you choose to study as your homework since the last meeting? Did you gain any special insights from this study? Were there any times when you felt the Spirit trying to speak to you? If so, can you share what the Spirit told you?

2. What other forms of prayer did you practice? Do you find that a particular form of prayer helps you to direct your attention to God? Are you praying the psalms or using the prayer of the quiet presence of God introduced in session 1?

3. Do you find that you have some major obstacle to prayer? What is that obstacle? What strategies can you think of to try to remove that obstacle?

4. Did you have any other spiritual insights or gifts since the last meeting?

review of some key points from previous sessions

Only God can enable us to share in the life of God. It is through union with Jesus Christ, who shares both our human nature and God's divine nature, that we can bridge the otherwise unbridgeable gap between God and us. The cross reminds us of God's desire to bring us to himself whatever the cost, if we will allow it to happen. It also reminds us that we must die to self so that Christ can live in us.

purpose of the fifth session

This session summarizes two stages of spiritual growth. In the first stage, we think of God as master and judge. In the second stage, we recognize that God is our friend, someone good who truly cares about us.

material for study and discussion

As we allow God to act within our lives, we grow spiritually; that is, our wills become more in harmony with God's will. We live less for ourselves and more for God. This is the most important aspect of our spiritual growth, since our love of God resides in the choices we make. We may sometimes think of love as being primarily a matter of the heart, which implies that love is a matter of how we feel, not what we do, but this is not so with divine love.

Nor, ultimately, does human love reside primarily in the emotions. Once the passions have cooled in a marriage, the partners must be willing to give of themselves to one another, sacrificing their own desires for the good of the family and for mutual support and happiness. Although there is a strong emotional content in married life, the proofs of love and the well-being of the union come from the choices the spouses make, not how they feel.

Some writers have tried to describe the stages that the soul passes through as it grows toward spiritual maturity. These stages are not to be taken as hard and fast, nor are the divisions between the stages always clear to those passing through them. In any case, we should never try to analyze how "holy" we are or how far the Spirit has brought us along the road to union with God. Our effort should concentrate on saying yes to God and opening ourselves to transforming grace, and then letting God take care of the rest. Nevertheless, a brief look at two of the stages of spiritual growth may be helpful.

The first stage of spiritual growth is called by some the *purgative* way. Those who live primarily for themselves and who have no desire to please God have not even entered this stage.

Generally, a stage of spiritual growth is characterized by the attitudes, actions, and forms of prayer of those involved in it. Someone who confuses an intermediate stage of spiritual growth with the ultimate goal of spiritual growth risks stagnation. Even if God then calls that person to a higher stage, he will resist the call, possibly even attributing the stirring of his mind, heart, and will to the devil. Likewise, a spiritual mentor who has a narrow view of spiritual growth can do terrible harm to a student who is seeking advice by telling the student that she ought not go where God is trying to lead her. We must always keep in mind that our goal is union with God in love, to know God intimately as God knows us, to love as we are loved. We will not reach this awesome goal in this life.

In the purgative way the soul recognizes the necessity of trying to obey the will of God, but the motive for so doing is either the fear of punishment for disobedience or the hope of a rich reward for obedience. God is primarily a distant and powerful authoritarian who demands that followers behave according to the rules set forth. Preachers who wish to scare listeners into conversion will graphically picture the horrors of hell, while preachers who wish to lure converts will seek to bribe listeners with the pleasures of heaven.

The soul in the purgative way wants rules to follow that show what to do to avoid divine punishment or what to do to gain divine favors. This soul wants clear guidelines, much like an unruly child must have, to know exactly what it can "get away with." The idea of God as a God of love and mercy is still very abstract and difficult to grasp.

Persons in the purgative way may be judgmental in their attitude toward others, since they assume that anyone who does not follow the same rules they are following must be sinning.

Prayer in the purgative way is usually according to some formula, either rote, read from Scripture or other inspirational sources, or following a particular pattern, generally using stock phrases even when it seems to be spontaneous. The reason these forms of prayer are used is that they are "safe." The person who uses them does not have to worry that these tried and true forms of prayer will bring trouble with God, even if they are not personally fulfilling. He or she may even feel drawn to speak to God on a more personal level, but is afraid to exercise that level of intimacy with the Almighty. This does not mean that persons at a more advanced spiritual level do not use prayers from Scripture or other written sources—even the eucharistic prayer follows a set pattern—but the bulk of prayer in the purgative way is really someone else's prayer rather than a prayer from the heart or an opening of the soul to God.

The purgative way depends more heavily on the emotions and senses than do later stages of the spiritual life. The will has been turned to God, but in a rather primitive and selfish way. One can easily become stuck in the purgative way because of the consolation of seemingly having clear rules that will lead to an eternal reward. There is little darkness and often little self-doubt in the purgative way, but there may also be little of the genuine experience of God. Someone in the purgative way will believe that God gave rules to test us. If we pass the test, we go to heaven; if we fail it, we go to hell.

The second stage of the spiritual life is called the *illuminative way*. Instead of being primarily concerned with avoiding sin in order to avoid punishment or gain reward, the soul wants to do good because doing good gratifies the soul and pleases God, who is now seen more as a dear friend than a vengeful judge. The soul recognizes God as good in himself, someone the soul wants to know more intimately. The soul is less worried about avoiding deliberate sin (since such avoidance now comes more easily) and more concerned about serving God because God is truly worth serving. The soul also wants to serve other human beings because God cares about them. When a soul in this stage does sin, there is sorrow at having let a friend down rather than fear that God will deal harshly with the sinner. The soul in this stage believes that God gave rules to help us to grow spiritually, much as a loving parent sets boundaries for children to teach and protect them.

The prayer in the illuminative way is more from the heart. One speaks to God as one would to a friend. The soul is willing to bare its deepest emotions, hopes and fears, and longings to God. The mind begins to dwell more on God in meditative prayer (a topic we will cover more fully in a later session).

review questions

1. What is characteristic of prayer in the purgative way?

2. What is characteristic of prayer in the illuminative way?

3. What are the principal motives for avoiding sin or doing good in the purgative way?

4. What is the principal motive that governs the choices of someone in the illuminative way?

additional questions for discussion

1. Would you try to obey God even if you did not believe in life after death? Why or why not?

2. Atheists think of life as a mere accident of nature having no real purpose or goal. Some Christians think of life as a time to test us to see if we are worthy to enter heaven. Others believe that life is a school in which we are to learn wisdom and love. What is your own view of the purpose of life?

3. How would you like the other members of the group to pray on your behalf? Ask the group to pray for you, and let each member voice a prayer in his or her own words for your intention.

homework assignment: an examination of our personal ministries

Thus far you have had homework exercises concerning prayer and study. Fidelity to the exercises helps to discipline and strengthen the will to serve God alone. Action is also an important part of our spiritual lives. Although spiritual growth depends on the work of the Spirit within us, God is usually preparing us to do something, to make our lives and actions his life and actions. Examine your actions during the time before the next session. Tell God, "I want all of my actions to be your actions." Pray that if God wishes to lead you in some direction, the Spirit will guide your mind to understanding what that might be. Try to see God's presence permeating your life and your work. You belong to God and you want to turn your life over to God, even as you continue in your current job and family situation. You want God to make your life a means of bringing you and your world into the life of God. Think carefully about this idea as you go about your work. Offer to God all that you do, so that God can make it his own.

To make this exercise more concrete, you might offer your entire day to God when you awake, asking that your actions be made a source of grace for yourself and for others. You might also pause periodically during the day to offer to God whatever you are doing.

SESSION 6
what's my spiritual bliss?

sharing of experiences and insights

1. Did you try to start each day by offering everything you will do that day to God? Did this make any difference in how you lived your day? Did you recall your consecration of your life to God at various times during the day? What other spiritual exercises did you practice (praying the psalms, a program of study, etc.)?

2. Did you have any special spiritual insights or experiences since the last meeting?

3. Have there been other forms of prayer or spiritual discipline not included as homework that you have started since this workshop began?

4. Since these sessions began, have you identified any particular issue that you believe is hindering your spiritual progress? What strategies have you adopted to try to address this issue in a positive way?

review of some key points from previous sessions

As we mature spiritually, we move from viewing God as a stern judge and master to seeing God as a friend who cares deeply about our welfare. We move from avoiding sin because we are afraid of hell or because we expect God to reward us to avoiding sin because it offends a loving friend. We move from viewing God's laws as a test we must pass to enter heaven to recognizing that these laws provide a framework within which the Spirit can best work in us to transform us into what God wants us to become.

purpose of the sixth session
This session introduces the concept of a *spirituality*. Basically, a spirituality is some aspect of divine truth on which we can focus as an aid to spiritual progress. Identifying a personal spirituality can assist us in formulating our "rule of life." The rule of life is discussed in later sessions.

material for study and discussion
What is a spirituality? Briefly, a spirituality is some aspect of divine truth that we find helpful in our quest for growth in the love of God; that is, some truth of our faith, or some model of the spiritual life, to which we feel strongly attracted.

Our faith is so rich that no human being, other than Christ alone, can encompass or express all of it in the way that he or she lives and relates to God. Likewise, no human being can reproduce in his or her own life all of the fullness of our Lord. Each person may have one or more special gifts, such as healing, or the ability to teach, or the ability to administer, or the ability to counsel those who are troubled, but no one exercises all of the spiritual gifts.

Likewise, in our spiritual lives, we do not find all of the truths of our faith equally valuable. The Trinity is more heavily stressed in Eastern Orthodoxy than in the West. Mary, the mother of Jesus, is venerated in Roman Catholicism and Orthodoxy, but is relatively ignored in most Protestant denominations. Some Christians are attracted to what they perceive to be the simplicity of the life of St. Francis of Assisi, while others admire the hidden, humble life of St. Teresa of the Child Jesus, a Roman Catholic nun who lived in obscurity until her death but who is considered by many theologians as the most important saint of modern times because of her "little way" of expressing her love of God.

The variety among those who have been venerated as saints by the church demonstrates that there are numerous roads to heroic sanctity, even though, in truth, there is still but one Way, which is Jesus Christ acting through the power of the Holy Spirit. The one Spirit who dwells in us all does not produce carbon copies of holiness. The kingdom of God displays a wonderful diversity. Each human being is unique in the mind of God. There was, and always will be, only one Francis of Assisi, and anyone who tries to slavishly mimic all of the characteristics of Francis's life will not achieve holiness, but may well go mad.

One might use the following analogy. Christ himself is a glorious diamond with innumerable facets, the members of his mystical body, the church. Each facet radiates with its own brilliance, adding to the luster of the whole. The radiance of the facet flows from being part of the diamond, illuminated by a splendid light, which is the Holy Spirit. No one facet is like any other facet, but all together they give the diamond its magnificent, luminous vitality.

Ultimately, of course, our life in God is expressed through love—love of God and love of our neighbor. But even in love, we cannot be all things. There are those who have expressed their love of God in lives of solitude in monasteries or convents. Others have worked among the poor. Still others have concentrated their charity on caring for the sick.

Although we generally think of love of God expressed in the life of those who have had special calls from God that have led them to the religious life, ordained ministry, or extraordinary work among the disadvantaged, we are all called to live our lives for God and to live our lives in love. The Great Commandment does not apply just to a few; it applies to all. Each of us must find that expression of our love of God that enables God to work most effectively in and through us. This means that each of us must identify the spirituality appropriate to our individual vocational calling.

Developing an individual spirituality does not mean that we deny any of the truths of our faith or that we deny our love to some for the sake of giving it to others. Rather, our love belongs first to God, and we exercise that love as the Spirit leads us. The circumstances of our lives are one important component of our spirituality. If we have a family, the odds are that we are not called to the monastic life. Our love of God and our neighbor must be reflected in our family life. If we do not love the members of our family in Christ, how, then, shall we love others?

Once we have, through prayer, reflection, and spiritual guidance, decided on a spirituality, that spirituality must be concretized in a "rule of life" (a subject we shall consider later on). The rule of life embodies our spirituality and determines how we shall live it. We must always keep in mind that neither a spirituality nor a rule of life is an end in itself, but only an additional means by which we can open our hearts and souls to allow God to transform us by the power of the Holy Spirit. We may think of a spirituality as choosing a spiritual location in which we can dwell most fruitfully, and we can think of a rule of life as the specific framework that governs our life in that location. We would have a different rule living in a desert than living in a city.

You might be wondering why one might want a particular spirituality. Here are two reasons. First, a personal spirituality helps give motivation and direction to prayer, study, and action. If we are interested in healing, for example, we will tend to read and pray about healing, and perhaps engage in a ministry related to healing. We will be less interested in books about the life of the desert fathers (and mothers), though the latter may be of interest if our spirituality concerns contemplative prayer. Second, a spirituality will help give focus to our rule of life, which otherwise might be hit or miss. Nevertheless, do not be too concerned about this for now. An appropriate spirituality will almost certainly emerge as you continue on your pilgrimage.

Here now are some examples of spiritualities. The examples are for illustration only. There may be as many examples of spiritualities as there are human beings.

✎ **A Creation Spirituality.** Many Christians—St. Francis of Assisi, for one—have been particularly attracted to God's glory reflected in creation. The prayer of someone who adopts this spirituality might focus on contemplating the beauty of nature. Study might include reading books on the environment. Action might include working to preserve the environment or volunteering at the SPCA.

✎ **A Spirituality of Music.** Music can be a sublime spiritual aid. The mind might be drawn to God by listening to popular or classical religious works, such as Brahms's German Requiem. Study might include practicing a musical instrument or taking voice lessons to gain or improve musical skills to be used in the service of God. Action can involve using musical talent in worship.

✎ **A Spirituality of Evangelism.** Although all Christians are called to spread the Good News, and thus be evangelists, some have a special aptitude for and interest in bringing others to Christ. Prayer here could include praying for the conversion of unbelievers or those who have lost their faith. Study could include works related to evangelism and action projects or programs to promote evangelization.

✎ **A Spirituality of Administration.** We might think of administration as primarily a secular activity, but Paul lists it as a gift of the Spirit (1 Corinthians 12:28). Someone gifted in administration can pray for the welfare of the program being administered and for God's guidance in running it, study in ways that will enhance personal administrative skills, and volunteer to organize and head church programs.

review questions

1. What is a spirituality?

2. Can you give two examples of a spirituality?

3. In what ways might having a spirituality be an aid to spiritual growth?

additional questions for discussion

1. Identify one or more possibilities for your own spirituality. Which seems most in line with your temperament as well as your present interests and circumstances?

2. Name a Christian you particularly admire. What is that individual's spirituality? Is it a spirituality to which you feel attracted and desire to emulate?

3. In what ways did Jesus exhibit the following spiritualities: a spirituality of poverty? a spirituality of teaching? a spirituality of compassion toward the suffering? What are some other spiritualities you can identify in Christ?

homework assignment: identify a personal spirituality

Bring to the next session descriptions of two or three spiritualities that particularly appeal to you. Are all of these possible spiritualities practical given your particular temperament and circumstances? Would you have to make any major changes in your lifestyle to adopt one or more of them? Think and pray carefully about your possible spirituality. You need not reach any definite conclusions now, but you should be reflecting on what your own spirituality might be and what adopting a particular spirituality might imply for your life. For example, your spirituality may involve "poverty in spirit." What does poverty mean to you? How does being poor in spirit differ from being materially poor? Your spirituality may center on the Lord's Supper, or on the spirituality of some great saint or hero of the church. But you would be wrong just to imitate someone else. Christ called you to become holy in your particular circumstances and with your particular personality and temperament. Though we are all meant to "become Christ," we do not do this by losing our individuality, but by being faithful disciples of our Lord.

SESSION 7
opening my mind to god through meditation*

sharing of experiences and insights

1. What material things are you most attached to? What would give you the most pain to give up if God asked you to do so? In what ways do you empty yourself so that Christ can fill you?

2. How do you seek to learn how Christ would have you reflect his love in your life? Are you "poor in spirit"?

3. What spiritualities did you choose as possibilities for your own spirituality? Why are these appealing to you? Which is most appealing?

4. Did you have any special spiritual insights or experiences since the last meeting?

review of some key points from previous sessions

A spirituality is some aspect of divine truth on which we can focus as an aid to spiritual progress. It is, in effect, the emphasis

---

*The group may decide to spend at least one session reviewing the first six sessions before continuing on. If you choose to do such a review, then session 7 will follow the review.

we choose as we try to let our lives reflect the life and love of Christ. What spirituality appeals most to us will depend on our personality and the circumstances of our lives.

purpose of the seventh session
In this session we look at meditation, a special method of directing our minds toward God and things related to God. What method of meditation is best suited for a person depends on that person's temperament.

material for study and discussion
Human beings have mental faculties: memory, intellect (reason), and will. Imagination is not a separate mental faculty, but instead involves drawing old images and ideas from memory in order to construct new ideas and images using our intellects.

We also have senses. The principal senses are touch, sight, hearing, smell, and taste. Our senses are the paths through which we collect information. Our mind processes and organizes the huge volume of data that comes to it from the senses. In addition, we have emotions, such as anger, fear, joy, and so forth. Having emotions, or feelings, is part of being human.

Meditation involves actively directing our memories and/or intellects toward God and things related to God. For example, we can deliberate on truths of our faith, events in the life of Christ, or an attribute of God, and try to draw lessons to apply to our lives. Rather than merely talking to God, as we do in many forms of prayer, we spend time in reflection.

This reflection does not have to be initiated in either the intellect or the memory. It might begin in the senses—for example, in looking at a sunset or smelling a flower, recognizing that God is mirrored in creation. Or the inspiration for meditation might come from a passage of Scripture or the words of a poem. What we use as the basis for our meditation depends to a great extent on our temperaments and our spirituality. For example, a musical performance (using the sense of hearing) may instill great joy (an emotion) that leads to reflection on the ability of human beings to share in the creative process with God (meditation on a truth of our faith). A session of meditation might close with a prayer that summarizes the thoughts or feelings produced by the meditation. Meditation might lead to an insight that prompts an act of the will, a choice, made because we have concluded that God wants us to make that choice.

Some people think best using mental images or pictures. Others are more verbal and think primarily using words. If I were to say the word "cat," some listeners would picture a cat in their minds, while others would conjure up words in their minds associated with "cat." Few if any people think entirely with images or entirely with words. But most people have one or the other as their principal mode of thought. One way of thinking is not better than another; they are simply different. But the way we think will heavily influence how we meditate.

Persons who are oriented toward verbal thought will usually prefer *discursive meditation*, which is primarily verbal and makes more use of the intellect. Persons who are oriented toward pictorial thought will usually prefer *imaginative meditation*, which makes greater use of the memory (and the imagination).

As noted, discursive meditation primarily involves our intellect or reason. Someone meditating in this way will ask questions related to a spiritual matter and try to answer them prayerfully. Such meditation may be initiated by first reading a passage from Scripture or other religious writing. You are invited to spend some time now practicing the following examples, one of discursive meditation and one of imaginative meditation. Note that both exercises begin with the same passage of Scripture, which is used as the inspiration. Although Scripture is often valuable to inspire meditation, we can, as noted earlier, enter meditation by other means.

Example of Discursive Meditation—

    ◈ *Passage on which to meditate:* "So Jesus called a little child to himself and set the child in front of them. Then he said, 'I tell you solemnly, unless you change and become like little children, you will never enter the kingdom of heaven.'"

    ◈ *Questions for reflection* (using the intellect to explore our relationship with God): What attributes do children have that would make Christ commend them to me as an example of how to live? Which of those attributes do I lack? What can I do to acquire or strengthen those attributes?

    ◈ *Closing prayer:* Lord, make me as a little child. I depend totally on you. I have nothing of my own, but all that I have that is good must come from you. Take me as your child and teach me all you would have me know. Amen.

Imaginative meditation involves the use of the imagination. Someone meditating in this manner will try to visualize in the eyes of the imagination a spiritual scene and then personally enter that scene. For example, one can sit at the Lord's feet with Mary, or kneel at the foot of the cross. This form of meditation, like discursive, can be inspired by reading a descriptive passage from Scripture or other religious text. It may also be inspired by looking at a religious picture. Spend time now in the practice of the following example of imaginative meditation.

Example of Imaginative Meditation—

    ◈ *Passage on which to meditate:* "So Jesus called a little child to himself and set the child in front of them. Then he said, 'I tell you solemnly, unless you change and become like little children, you will never enter the kingdom of heaven.'"

☙ *Questions for reflection* (setting the scene and placing yourself in it): Imagine Jesus standing in a group of people. Set the scene carefully. How are he and the others in the scene dressed? What kind of day is it? Are there houses nearby, or is it a broad, open area? Imagine a little child running up to Jesus. Is the child happy or sad? Place yourself in the scene. You can be anyone you want to be. You can even be Jesus welcoming and blessing the child. Enjoy the scene. Is anyone saying something? Is Jesus speaking to you? What is he saying?

☙ *Closing prayer:* Beloved Jesus, help me to see you always present in my life. Let me be free to come to you as a little child. Bless me and let me remain with you always. Amen.

Note that even in the example of imaginative meditation we included words. Words are not required, however, and we might have been content simply to stand quietly in Jesus' presence or look lovingly into his face.

Discursive and imaginative forms of meditation both can be useful and powerful sources of inspiration and of learning more about ourselves and our relationship to God. Nevertheless, some warnings must be given.

1. We may become so attached to the pleasure and emotional highs obtained from meditation that we lose sight of the purpose for which we meditate: to open our minds and hearts to the action of God. God is always the goal. Neither prayer nor even Scripture is an end in itself. Both are means to allow God to bring us into union with himself.

2. We may lead ourselves astray by erroneous thoughts gathered during these meditations, mistaking our own preferences for the promptings of God. We should be wary of any messages that come "directly from God." If we are prompted to unusual actions or beliefs, these should be tested through prayer and with a trusted spiritual adviser.

3. Beware of pride. Gaining great consolations and "mountaintop experiences" from meditation can lead someone to think that he or she has arrived at a high level of holiness. But our goal is to come to a knowledge of God—to know God himself—not just a knowledge *about* God. God is not known through the intellect or imagination, much less through the emotions. Keep in mind that holiness is in the choices we make, not in our feelings. If your prayer, whatever form it may take, does not lead to a deeper desire to please God and serve others, you should examine carefully whether you are praying for personal satisfaction rather than to open yourself to God.

While most people are either predominantly verbal or predominantly visual—that is, they think primarily in words or primarily in pictures—few people are purely one or the other. Thus, you might be best mixing images and words in your meditation—for example, placing yourself in a scene and then listening to the conversations of others, or carrying on a conversation yourself with one of the characters in the scene. It would not even be blasphemous to place yourself in the role of Christ to try to experience how he might have felt or what he might have said. Our emotions can be not only the inspiration for meditation, but can also enter into the meditation itself. Resting in a beautiful scene or listening intently to a magnificent piece of music, giving glory to God for creation or the creative spirit of the human mind, can also be a powerful meditative prayer. Do not be afraid to experiment with different forms and styles of meditation to find one that fits your own temperament particularly well.

review questions

1. What is meditation?

2. How can the senses serve as inspiration for meditation?

3. What is the difference between discursive meditation and imaginative meditation?
4. Does holiness of life consist in being able to meditate well? In what does holiness of life consist?

additional questions for discussion

1. Which form of thought do you lean toward, verbal or pictorial? Does the answer depend on what you are thinking about? Does it change from time to time?
2. Which of the meditative exercises did you find easier? What obstacles to meditating did you have in each exercise? How might these be lessened?
3. What forms of inspiration for meditation do you think would work best for you? Have you actually engaged in meditation before but did not know it was called meditation?

homework assignment: practice meditation

Spend at least ten minutes every day practicing meditative prayer. The inspiration and theme for your meditation is up to you. You might, for example, use one of your favorite Scripture passages. In discursive meditation you might then ask yourself questions that force you to apply the passage to your own life. Be open to the Spirit's guidance.

For imaginative meditation, visualize a scene and place yourself in it. What is your response to being a part of that action? If Jesus or some other holy person is there, what do you say to him or her? What do they say to you?

Experiment with different forms of meditation and different means to inspire meditation. You might also look in a bookstore for a suitable collection of meditations. Bookstores that reflect the rich meditative tradition of Roman Catholicism are particularly good resources in which to find such collections.

SESSION 8
three key virtues

sharing of experiences and insights

1. Did you try to meditate since the last session? If so, what method or methods did you find most helpful? What means did you use to begin your meditation—reading Scripture, listening to music, or something else? What means was most successful? What were your principal obstacles to meditation? What strategies did you use to try to remove those obstacles? What else can you and the group suggest that might help you to meditate (e.g., use a different means to inspire you, focus your attention on a holy picture or object, have quiet music in the background)?

2. Have you continued any of the other exercises that have been assigned? If you have not been continuing any of the exercises assigned for each session, what has prevented you from doing so? Have you substituted other exercises that you found more valuable?

3. Have you had any special spiritual insights or experiences since the last session?

review of some key points from previous sessions

Our goal is to share in the life of God so that we can know God as God knows us. Only through the Spirit working in us can we achieve this goal. But God will move us toward this goal if we surrender control to and cooperate with God rather than attempting to do the work ourselves. In meditation we focus our minds on some aspect of our faith, and we seek a deeper understanding of how God is acting in our lives and how best to respond to God's action.

purpose of the eighth session
We will explore the theological virtues, virtues that we must cultivate in order to grow spiritually. We will then relate these virtues to our mental faculties.

material for study and discussion
As human beings we have bodies and minds as well as souls. Our bodies are the means by which we interact with the physical universe. We experience and learn primarily through our senses, processing in our minds the data that the senses provide. Without the senses we would have no natural way to acquire new data about the world around us, or to come to know anything new.

Our minds have at least three faculties: the intellect, by which we reason and understand; the will, by which we choose; and the memory, by which we store data that was first received from the senses, but which is usually then processed by the intellect. The memory is also responsible for our imaginations, since we draw on images in the memory to construct the objects that we create with our imagination.

There are three *theological virtues*: faith, hope, and charity. These are related to the faculties of the mind, but, as we shall see, they necessarily transcend, or surpass, them.

We note first that we cannot know God through the senses. We cannot taste God, smell God, hear God, see God, or touch

God. We can know and experience things related to God through the senses—for example, we can hear beautiful liturgical music and see magnificent sacred art—but none of these things is God. Even the intrinsic beauty of a sunset, or of a baby, or of anything we can sense, is not God. If it were God, God would be finite, a creature like ourselves, able to be contained within a small portion of our universe. Whatever we can sense cannot be God.

Nor can we know God with our intellect. Our intellect ultimately gains its knowledge from the senses. Moreover, whatever can be contained in our intellect is necessarily finite. No matter how exalted our thoughts may be, or how educated we are, we cannot know or understand God through our intellects. Knowing God soars far above the power of human reason.

And since whatever is found in the memory ultimately is traceable back to sensory data, we cannot know God through the memory. No matter how wonderful our memories may be, or how grand and inspiring may be the products of our imaginations, none of these enable us to know God directly.

As human beings dependent on our senses for knowledge as well as pleasure, we may become inordinately attached to sensory impressions. We love to hear certain music because it gives us a "glow" that we may assume is the presence of God. We love to look at certain pictures because they remind us of the joy we felt during some "mountaintop experience." We love to recite certain prayers because of the deep emotional impact that they have on us. But no matter how deeply we are affected by our senses or emotions, or even by what we experience through the faculties of our minds, we are not thereby experiencing God.

To know God, to experience God, we must eventually put aside both the bodily senses and the faculties of our minds. We do not, we cannot, approach God through naturally acquired knowledge, even naturally acquired knowledge about God. We do not approach God through knowing but through unknowing—not through natural light, but through divine darkness.

If we are to experience God directly, we cannot do so through the senses or through our mental faculties, because such experience lies beyond their powers. God must work with the soul to allow the soul to experience God directly. The more we cling to the senses or to our mental images of God, the more we restrain God from raising us to a truer and deeper knowledge of him. We must not only become poor in spirit, in the sense of recognizing that all our material possessions are only loaned to us by God to use in his service, but also must become poor by leaving aside even those things that can give us some of our greatest natural pleasure: our senses and our mental faculties.

If we cannot know God by natural means, then how can we come to a knowledge of God? We do so by the virtue of faith. Faith informs our intellect by surrendering it to complete trust in God. Like Abraham, we must leave the land we know to go to a land that only God can show us, and that we cannot come to know by our own powers. We do not even know where to look, but we have faith that God will take us there and reveal the promised land to us. We are emptying ourselves of all in which we previously trusted to place our faith in God alone. We enter into the darkness of "blind faith" to find what cannot be naturally understood. We must be willing to let go of all that we can grasp through our natural abilities in order to abandon ourselves into the hands of God to lift us to levels that we could not approach on our own. We must enter a "cloud of unknowing," as one writer calls it, that we may have a purer faith and a purer knowledge of the One Who Cannot Be Known, the One Who Simply Is.

Hope also sustains us in our pilgrimage. Whereas faith is a present trust in the love and mercy of an unseen God, hope looks to the future. Hope is the certainty that what God has promised, God will bring about. God has promised to bring us into union with him if we will allow it. Hope sustains us in the often difficult journey to the fulfillment of that promise. Faith looks to the present; hope looks to the future.

Faith, related to our memory, remembers God's revelation and clings to it with confidence, knowing that God can be trusted. We have faith because God is faithful. Hope is related to our intellect or reason, because through the intellect we understand that we can have complete confidence in God. Faith and hope are called theological virtues because they have God and God's self-revelation as their object.

Charity, or love of God and of others in God, is the greatest of the theological virtues. Charity is a function of the will. We conform our wills to what we believe God wants of us. We do what we believe God wants us to do so that we may be more completely one with God.

It is through charity that we become conformed to God and become "perfect." Remember that Christ was perfect because he always did the will of his Father. Christ's life was a life of perfect love of God, and we should ask God to make our lives into lives of perfect love as well.

Paul reminds us that when we see God face to face, we will have no need of either faith or hope. God will have fulfilled all promises, and we will experience God directly. But then our love will be perfected. We will be conformed to God, made one with God, as much as a creature can be made one with God by the divine power itself. Our wills shall be inseparable, indeed, indistinguishable from God's will. Charity will reach its perfect fulfillment in heaven.

review questions

1. What are the three theological virtues? What are their definitions?

2. What are the three faculties of the mind?

3. How are the mental faculties related to the three theological virtues?

4. What is the only theological virtue that will continue into eternity? Why?

additional questions for discussion

1. In addition to memory, reason, and will, humans have a characteristic that seems utterly unique to humanity: self-consciousness. We not only know, but also are aware that we know. We recognize ourselves as distinct individuals. Another example of a characteristic apparently unique to human beings is the ability to appreciate music. What are some other characteristics that appear to be unique to human beings?

2. What are the implications of self-consciousness for spiritual growth? For example, if we were not self-conscious, would we be able to recognize the difference between good and evil? Would we be aware that someday each of us must die?

3. How is faith defined as "accepting a statement as true because God has revealed it" different from faith as complete trust in God? Can we have one form of faith without the other? Which form of faith is more important for spiritual growth? Why?

homework assignment: reflect on certain questions

For the next session, reflect on the following questions: How much do you depend on your senses or your emotions for your practice of religion—for example, by demanding emotional satisfaction from your prayer practices? How much do you depend on your intellect for your practice of religion—for example, by refusing to accept anything you cannot understand?

How willing are you to let God take complete control of your life, even if this means giving up the dependencies identified earlier? What is there about your life that you most want to retain control over? Offer your desire to remain in control of your life to God in love, asking to be taught true poverty of spirit. Write a short summary of your responses to these questions to share with the group at the next meeting. Continue a daily practice of prayer and study.

SESSION 9
structuring life
to help spiritual growth

sharing of experiences and insights

1. What experiences or exercises in your spiritual life give your senses or emotions the most pleasure? What experiences would you be most reluctant to give up? How willing are you to trust God completely to bring you to himself even if this process meant giving up much of your sensory or emotional pleasure?

2. What in your life do you feel you most need to control? Over what do you feel the least control? Would you be willing to pray as follows: "Lord, take from me whatever separates me from you even if you must take it by force"? Why or why not?

3. Which of the other exercises previously assigned have you been practicing on a regular basis? Which have been the most difficult and which the most satisfying? Why?

4. Have you had any special insights since the last meeting?

review of some key points from previous sessions

We bring our complete humanness to our spiritual lives, including our minds, emotions, and senses. All of these components of our humanness can aid us to direct our thoughts and actions to God, to consecrate our entire life to God. But we must always remember that the goal is God himself, and only God can bring us to this goal. God will do so if we accept the invitation to come into union with God and open ourselves to the Spirit's transforming work in us.

purpose of the ninth session
The notion of a "rule of life" is introduced. A rule of life helps us to focus on God and is an aid to being more open to God.

material for study and discussion
We recall once more that it is only through God's action that we can come to know God directly. We are assured by Jesus himself that God wants to bring us to the knowledge of him, but in order for this to happen, we must be open to what God wants to do for us. We must not only say yes to God, but also place our hearts and minds and souls and strength at his disposal, humbly offering all that we have and are and do, asking to be drawn through Christ into God's own divine life by the power of the Holy Spirit.

With this thought in mind, we began the practice of certain exercises that included prayer, study, and action to show our sincerity in saying yes to God and to provide openings for God to act in us. These exercises do not follow a pattern. They were introduced just to give a sample, and only a small sample at that, of various kinds of spiritual practices. If some of the practices were helpful, well and good. If not, there is no reason to be discouraged. Each person must find a spiritual program that is suited to his or her individual temperament and circumstances. Experimentation is encouraged.

Nevertheless, each seeker should have a basic program to follow consistently that forms a foundation for opening him or her more fully to God. This basic program is the *rule of life*. Some people do not like the idea of a rule, so if it helps to call it a "framework of life" or something else, do so. But the idea is one of central importance for spiritual progress.

A rule of life should be carefully and prayerfully constructed, but with the clear understanding that adjustments can be made as necessary; indeed, the rule of life may require adjustments as one progresses in the spiritual life. For example, meditation may yield to passive contemplative prayer, a foretaste of the direct vision of God, should God grant that grace.

What you decide to do as part of your rule of life is entirely up to you. Here, below, and in the next session, we give suggestions for formulating your rule. Your rule should by no means try to contain all that you do for God. Hopefully, your whole life is lived for God. Rather, your rule consists of practices that you make a special commitment to carry out. When you do an activity that is part of your rule of life, you should remind yourself that you are engaging in that activity to say yes to the invitation to allow God to bring you into union with him, and that you are opening yourself as best you can to what God wants to do for you.

A good rule of life must fit your circumstances and temperament. No benefit will come from resolving to do more than you have time for, nor should you attempt a particular task that would be extraordinarily difficult to complete, unless there is substantial reason to believe that God is leading you to attempt it.

Although it is true that if you try to do too much, you may become discouraged, and even abandon the quest for a deeper spiritual life, it is also true that making too small an investment by constructing a rule of life with minimal content might slow your spiritual development. You should try to do as much as you reasonably can in your particular circumstances, recognizing that growth into God must be the highest priority in your life. Remember that you are committing yourself to carry out your rule, even if you must give up another spiritual practice in favor of one that is part of your rule.

Some will say that they do not have the energy left after a draining day at work or with the press of personal crises to do anything substantial. Remember, however, that it is not you who must do the work. You are to let God do the work, and you must have faith that God will do the work if you allow it. This means that you must press on even when you feel utterly dry and incapable of prayer.

You are to be faithful to your rule even when you seem to be beating your head against a wall. If you do find that your rule of life is causing you emotional distress or that following it creates serious tension or anxiety, then you will need to consider what changes need to be made to your rule to bring it more into line with your temperament and circumstances. The group may be able to assist you in this regard if it decides to continue for group spiritual direction. The problem in many cases is not that an individual cannot pray, but has certain expectations about what should happen when he or she does pray (consolations, emotional highs, etc.), and when these expectations are not met, the individual thinks that time is being wasted or that prayer is not being done properly. No true prayer is ever a waste of time, nor is any action a waste of time if it is done with the sincere intention of pleasing God.

You should pick components for your rule that will not become rote drills. You are not adopting a rule to score points, but to say yes to God and to open your soul to him. Exercises done in the wrong spirit—for example, in a perfunctory manner—can close the soul rather than open it.

Nor should time be an issue. As you will see, there are numerous exercises that do not take time away from your necessary work, and some that even save you time. Generally, a rule contains activities in three areas: prayer, study, and action (ministry). Here are some examples of what might be included in each part of your rule. Again, these are intended only as samples or suggestions. You are the one who determines what your rule will be.

✎ **Prayer:** Quiet presence of God; consecrating your day to God when you wake up; offering your work (play, sleep, etc.) to God by asking that it be used in his service; a form of meditation that best suits your style and temperament; praying the psalms.

✎ **Study:** Reading from Scripture or religious works; religious education opportunities; study groups.

✎ **Action:** Prayers for the success of evangelism; prayers for the needs of others; fasting; acts of commission and omission offered in love for God; seeking to bring friends and neighbors to Christ; working for the Lord through the church or other agencies.

An example of a simple rule of life would be the following:

✎ Say a prayer consecrating my day to God when I wake up in the morning.

✎ Read one chapter from a Gospel sometime each day.

✎ Drive weekly for the "Meals on Wheels" program.

Each element of your rule must be sufficiently precise in terms of what to do and when or how often to do it that you can evaluate whether you are faithfully carrying out that element. "Think good thoughts daily" may be sufficiently clear about when, but it is fuzzy about what to do. "I will say the Lord's Prayer when I feel like it" is clear about what to do, but it is fuzzy about when or how often; moreover, it makes no real commitment, because it requires saying the Lord's Prayer only when the person feels like doing so. "I will say at least one Lord's Prayer every other day" is precise about both what to do and when or how often to do it.

Do not try to pile all of your activities into your rule of life. The rule should include a basic minimum of spiritual exercises that you will faithfully carry out. And when you do these exercises, you are to intentionally remind yourself that you are saying yes to God's invitation to come into union with him in love and that you are trying to open yourself to God's transforming grace.

review questions

1. Describe "rule of life" in your own words.

2. Should you go to your priest or minister to get your rule of life? Why or why not?

3. What are the areas from which the contents of a rule of life are often chosen?

4. In what ways must an activity contained in a rule of life be well defined?

5. With what specific intentions should you carry out an activity that is part of your rule of life?

additional questions for discussion

1. What signs lead me to believe that God is active in my life?

2. If God calls every human being into union with him, why do so many seem unaware of this divine invitation? What means could we use to make others more aware of the invitation to know God?

3. If I sense that God seems to be calling me to some unusually difficult activity, what means can I use to determine if that call is truly from God?

homework assignment: begin to design your rule of life

Begin to formulate a rule of life, one that includes components of prayer, study, and action. The components of your rule must be workable for you and be true to your own interests and character as well as your circumstances. You alone ultimately must decide what is appropriate for you, although you may seek counsel from Scripture, prayer, and spiritual advisers. Never adopt a rule just because it seems to be working for someone else. Your rule must be your rule and no one else's. Experiment with living your rule once you have designed it. Reexamine your rule in light of what you experience in living it.

SESSION 10
more about a "rule of life"

sharing of experiences and insights

1. Have you made progress toward formulating a rule of life? What prayer practice or practices have you included in your rule? Did you have any problems in composing a rule of life, and, if so, how did you address them? (Note: the group is never to judge whether someone's rule is right or wrong. If someone is having trouble with some particular part of his or her rule, the group may suggest trying an alternative to what is not working, but it is solely a personal decision what a person's rule of life should include.

2. Does the idea of having a "rule" and sticking to it bother you, and, if so, why?

3. What is your principal form of prayer now? Has your mode of prayer changed since you began this program?

4. Have you had any special spiritual insights or experiences since the last meeting?

review of some key points from previous sessions

A rule of life generally contains components related to prayer, study, and ministry. Each component must be sufficiently clear in terms of what to do and when or how often to do it so that someone can tell whether the component has been completed.

purpose of the tenth session

We continue our discussion of the rule of life, emphasizing key points made in session 9 and elaborating on the reason for having a rule of life.

material for study and discussion

A rule of life can be a powerful aid in spiritual growth. Without some clear direction and structure to our spiritual walk, we are likely to wander aimlessly, trying this path and that, depending on what strikes our fancy at the moment or what seems to give the greatest emotional high. Without a rule, we may simply do nothing at all, because we have not committed ourselves to certain exercises each and every day. The rule of life focuses our efforts and provides greater assurance that we will continue to open ourselves to God's action. If we are practicing the rule with the proper intention, we continually remind ourselves that we have accepted God's invitation to come into union with him, and we open ourselves to the Spirit to mold us as God chooses.

To be effective, a rule of life must fit the individual's personality and circumstances. The rule of life for a homemaker is unlikely to be a workable rule for an automobile mechanic. This is not because the homemaker's rule is better or worse than the mechanic's, but because the circumstances in which a homemaker operates are significantly different from those of someone who repairs automobiles. When constructing a rule of life, do not guess what your minister or the group wants from you, and much less should you think about what would impress others. Your rule is something that you must be able to live with. If your rule is not suited to your own personality and circumstances, you will quickly become discouraged because you will not be able to keep such a rule, or the rule will not provide God adequate opportunity to transform you. The rule, after all, is not an end in itself. It is to provide structure to your life so that God can work more easily with and in you.

This means that your rule must be based on self-knowledge. Moreover, if your rule is a good one, it will lead to further self-knowledge. Growth in the life of God must be founded in truth, since God is truth. We cannot deceive God, no matter how well we may deceive others or ourselves. If a rule is an attempt to bolster a false self-image or make us appear more holy to others or even to ourselves, our rule can be a spiritual trap rather than a spiritual aid.

Your rule should generally be based on your personal spirituality. Perhaps you still are not clear about what your spirituality is. If you have a good rule, it will help clarify and define your spirituality. We cannot reflect all of the attributes of Christ or the goodness of God. We must concentrate our attention on those aspects of our faith that most attract and interest us, the aspects that define our spirituality. If we are drawn toward a healing ministry, for example, we might emphasize study and action related to healing. Or if we are raising children, we might be attracted to the childlike qualities needed to enter the kingdom of heaven, or to Christ's love of little children. Nevertheless, even if you do not have a clear spirituality when you develop a rule of life, a spirituality is likely to emerge before long. At that time, your rule can be adjusted to take your developing spirituality into account. And this brings up another point.

While a rule of life is important, it is unlikely to be a rule *for* life; that is, it will change as you change, or as God changes you. The type of prayer that is appropriate and helpful to a beginner may impede progress for someone whom God has chosen to draw into another form of prayer. The emphasis in your ministry may change as new opportunities present themselves or as the Spirit makes God's intention clearer for you. While you can almost certainly profit from having a rule of life, you might not always have the same rule of life. But when should you change your rule, and how do you know if the rule you have chosen is appropriate for you?

At any stage of your spiritual development, spiritual direction, or at least some form of spiritual friendship, is important. The next session deals with that important topic. Before we go on in this session, however, we review some fundamental principles about rules of life.

1. Each element of your rule of life must be well defined in terms of action and time. An element is well defined if you can determine whether or not you have satisfied it.

>—*Examples of action*
>
>**Okay:** dedicate the day to God; say the Lord's Prayer; receive Communion
>
>**Not okay:** be a good person; think kind thoughts
>
>—*Examples of time*
>
>**Okay:** upon waking in the morning; three times a day; once a week; before each meal
>
>**Not okay:** occasionally; once in awhile; when I feel like it

2. A rule of life includes only specific elements you commit to carry out on a regular and continuing basis. It cannot, and should not, encompass everything you do related to prayer and the practice of your faith.

3. Consistent failure to follow through on some element of your rule of life may be due to one or more reasons—for example, a poorly designed rule; lack of commitment; impossibility of performance. But you must always be accountable in your practice of your rule, trying honestly to determine whether or not you are practicing the rule, and if not, why.

4. A rule of life is not practiced for its own sake but to demonstrate your sincere commitment to say yes to God and to give God opportunities to transform the soul. If the rule becomes an end in itself, it will fail its intended purpose. Remind yourself frequently why you have a rule and ask God to guide you in its practice.

5. Because accountability is necessary to keep you honest in your practice of the rule, and because the rule often must change as your circumstances change, spiritual direction is an important complement to the practice of a rule. Session 11 will look more closely at the benefits of such spiritual direction.

review questions

1. With what intentions should you practice your rule of life?

2. If you find it too difficult or anxiety-producing to carry out the rule of life you adopted, what should you do?

3. Is your current rule of life likely to be your rule for the rest of your life?

4. What is an important complement to practicing a rule?

5. If someone else is doing less for his or her rule than you are doing for yours, should you suggest to that person to do more? Why or why not?

additional questions for discussion

1. In what ways is being part of a faith community likely to help in the practice of your rule? What difficulties does one face trying to grow spiritually in isolation?

2. Taking care of your health, for example, by exercising a specific amount during the week, can also be part of your rule of life. Why can such seemingly secular activities as exercise reasonably form part of a spiritual rule?

3. Have you identified your spirituality yet? If so, what is it, and why does it appeal to you?

homework assignment: finish defining your rule of life

Complete your rule of life. It should include components from: (1) prayer; (2) study, in order to develop your mind for ministry and to give God greater opportunity to inform your intellect; and (3) ministry, in order to advance the kingdom and carry on the work of Christ. This ministry does not necessarily have to be active work in the community. It could be a prayer ministry for the church and the community, or being certain that your children receive proper religious instruction. Practice your rule. Make written notes on any issues that arise concerning this practice—for example, difficulties, spiritual insights received while practicing the rule, adjustments you have had to make to your life to practice the rule, or adjustments to your original rule to make it more workable.

SESSION 11
it helps to have
a traveling companion

sharing of experiences and insights

1. Now that you have developed a rule of life, are you consciously and intentionally keeping it? If you are not, why? What problems or concerns prevent you from doing so? If you have not been able to keep your rule, your problem may be one of the following: (a) the rule is so vague that you cannot tell whether you are keeping it or not; (b) the rule includes too much for you to fit reasonably into your schedule; (c) the rule is not well designed for your particular temperament or circumstances; (d) you have not really made keeping the rule a high priority.

2. Have you had any special spiritual experiences or insights since the last session?

3. Did you learn anything new about yourself as you were composing your rule of life?

review of some key points from previous sessions

A rule of life should help you to renew periodically your acceptance of the invitation to share in God's own life and to be more open to God's transforming grace. A rule must not be adopted to score spiritual points or to make you appear to be more religious.

purpose of the eleventh session

This session explores what spiritual direction is and is not, and how it can be an aid for spiritual growth.

material for study and discussion

Someone trying to live a rule of life in order to be as open to God as possible will usually find at least four things valuable in this effort: (1) accountability; (2) aid in identifying how God is acting in his or her life; (3) formulating an appropriate response to God's action once that action is identified; and (4) receiving encouragement and prayer support. Spiritual direction should include all four of these components.

If we have a rule of life or are simply trying to be faithful to God's will without a rule but need not tell anyone else how we are doing, or if we are in fact doing what we have committed to do, then we are accountable only to ourselves. Twelve-step groups derive much of their benefit from the fact that a member must report successes or failures to the group. Likewise, if we have no one to whom we report our spiritual successes or failures, we may soon drop any pretense of trying to progress spiritually. Accountability helps keep us honest and on track.

Generally, spiritual direction is not a forum in which we confess sins. Failing to keep a rule of life is not a sin in the traditional sense of knowingly and intentionally violating a law of God, since a rule of life is not a commandment but a spiritual aid. But we are more likely to be faithful to our rule if we must tell others, even in a confidential and supportive environment, how we have been doing with our rule.

Few people are so well in touch with, and sufficiently objective concerning, themselves that they can always discern God's actions in their lives, or discerning that action, can formulate an appropriate response on their own. Often, when confronted with a choice concerning work or family, we discuss the matter first with family members, trusted friends, or professional advisers to better define the issues involved and to explore alternatives before making a decision. Why, then, should the matter be different with spiritual decisions?

Humans are social beings and frequently find support and strength within a community. At the least, we need others to offer encouragement and to lift us up in prayer. Spiritual growth is not a do-it-yourself job. The risk of deceiving ourselves or losing resolve is greater when we go it alone without others to accompany and support us on our pilgrimage. Someone who claims to be walking alone with Christ may someday find that he or she is simply walking alone. Following his ascension, Christ has chosen to carry on his ministry through the members of his body, the church. We ignore this truth at our spiritual peril.

What, then, is a spiritual director? It is an individual (or a group), the director, who provides the assistance outlined above to the seeker, the directee. What the director provides to the directee is spiritual direction. Some people object to the term "spiritual director" because they do not think that a director should really direct, but rather, be a loving and patient listener who helps the directee come to his or her own conclusions. Therefore, they use a different term, such as "spiritual guide" or "spiritual mentor." What you call the person is not as important as what that individual actually does. Certainly, it is helpful to have trustworthy persons with whom you can talk comfortably about your spiritual life, but it is even more helpful when these same persons can give you sound advice based on study, experience, and common sense to support you in your pilgrimage.

Therefore, being a spiritual director, in my understanding of the role, involves more than just lending a willing and compassionate ear and praying with the directee. The director is someone who assists the directee in formulating a rule of life and in making appropriate adjustments to that rule, helping the directee discern signs of God working and how to respond appropriately, and aiding the directee in addressing concerns and problems that arise in the spiritual life. The director may also recommend readings, exercises, workshops, and the like that he or she believes may benefit the directee. In other words, spiritual direction involves actual directing, at least in the sense of providing positive suggestions. A directee usually goes to a spiritual director in the belief that the director can provide information that the directee does not yet have. The director, then, by implication, is someone who knows at least as much about spiritual development as the directee and can assist in finding those methods related to spiritual growth that are most appropriate in light of the directee's disposition and circumstances.

What, then, are the attributes that qualify someone to be a spiritual director? Ordination in itself is not a qualification. Unfortunately, many ministers and priests have little spiritual formation. They might be well educated in theology and Scripture but have minimal experience that would prepare them to become spiritual directors. Moreover, many ministers have little time for or interest in serving as spiritual directors.

There are several hundred institutes and courses of study in the United States alone that lead to certification in spiritual direction, but even certification from one of these is no guarantee that someone will make a competent spiritual director. First, no uniform guidelines or standards for such programs exist, nor does universal agreement on the nature of spiritual direction or the personal attributes, experience, or knowledge required of spiritual directors. Obviously, someone who considers direction to be a form of therapy will disagree on this matter with someone who considers a director to be simply a good listener, and both of them will disagree with someone who thinks that the director can actually help steer the directee toward greater spiritual progress.

I believe the most important characteristics of a spiritual director are these:

1. The director must be someone with whom the directee feels personally comfortable, a person the directee is willing to trust with innermost thoughts. Even if a director is otherwise splendidly qualified, the directee cannot be helped if, for reasons good or bad, he or she feels uncomfortable with the director.

2. The director must be someone willing and able to recognize that the Spirit breathes as it will and that the director's way is not the only way to union with God. A director must be open to prayerful discernment of where God is leading a directee, as opposed to where the director might choose to lead. Put another way, the director must treat each directee as an individual and seek to let the spiritual direction ministry reflect the mind of God rather than personal biases. The director must also have the humility to recognize that many directees may well be more advanced spiritually than he or she is. And a director must adopt the medical profession's primary rule: Do no harm.

3. The director should be experienced in the spiritual life rather than merely versed in the literature and theory of the spiritual life; yet, the director must have some theological grounding in order to avoid falling inadvertently into serious error and to be able to communicate theological concepts more clearly. Without extensive actual experience of the spiritual life, a director will be constructing mental images of what a spiritual life ought to be and risks substituting imagination for reality. It is like a person who, having read a book about how to fly an airplane, claims to be a pilot.

4. The director should be a person of prayer, recognizing that he or she is merely an imperfect instrument of God through whom the Spirit must act if the direction is to be helpful to the directee.

5. The director must be able to keep any and all confidences absolutely inviolate.

It is not easy to find a suitable spiritual director. There may be retreat houses and religious communities in the area that offer spiritual direction, and some churches may have persons on staff who practice spiritual direction, but finding a person who has the characteristics of a good director and with whom the directee feels comfortable can be difficult. Nevertheless, spiritual direction can be extremely useful for spiritual growth, and there are steps someone can take if an individual director is not available. The group itself, for example, can become a spiritual director for its members. We will explore this idea in the next part of this book.

To summarize some specific ways in which a spiritual director can be helpful:

1. Assist with a neutral but compassionate ear to help the directee discern God's leading and how to respond appropriately to the promptings of the Spirit.

2. Be a reality check for the directee. Part of this role is making the directee accountable in such matters as observance of the directee's rule of life.

3. Provide the directee with concrete resources and practical suggestions related to the directee's own circumstances and deepening spirituality.

4. Pray with and for the directee.

review questions

1. What are four services that a spiritual director should perform for a directee?

2. What are at least three characteristics that a good spiritual director should have?

3. Is there a generally recognized training program that a person must complete to qualify as a spiritual director? Are persons trained for the ordained ministry always qualified to be spiritual directors?

4. Does the fact that someone is well qualified as a spiritual director necessarily mean that that person would make a good director for you?

additional questions for discussion

1. Name someone who was especially influential in forming you spiritually. What characteristics did this person have that were helpful in your formation?

2. A spiritual director must be compassionate, recognizing that all human beings are imperfect. However, would you prefer a director who called attention to what he or she thought was wrongful behavior on your part, or a director who was nonjudgmental and who let you form your own conclusions about what was right and wrong for you?

3. Do you feel that this group has given you spiritual direction as you have proceeded through the sessions? Would you feel comfortable allowing this group to continue as your spiritual director(s) once the sessions are finished?

homework assignment: keeping notes on your rule of life

Pay attention to your feelings and experiences as you live your rule of life. Keep a written record for one week of any problems you have in keeping the rule. Also note any special insights about God or yourself that you have during that time. Do any parts of your rule now strike you as impractical or not appropriate for your temperament or circumstances? Which parts have been the most difficult to carry out? What are the principal obstacles you have had to overcome to be faithful to your rule? How did you overcome them, or do you feel that you are still struggling with the obstacles?

SESSION 12
more about spiritual direction

sharing of experiences and insights

1. Read to the group what you wrote concerning your experience with your rule since the last session. Are any changes in your rule called for because of your observations?

2. Have you learned anything about prayer practices that you were not aware of before you began these sessions?

3. Did you have any special spiritual insights or experiences since the last session?

review of some key points from previous sessions

A spiritual director is someone who will help another person, the directee, to discern how God is acting in the directee's life and how to respond appropriately to that action. The director may also suggest resources (such as books or workshops) that might help the directee, and will support the directee with prayer.

purpose of the twelfth session

In this session we explore what spiritual direction is not, look again at the attributes of a good director, and discuss the attitudes that a directee should bring to direction.

material for study and discussion

Spiritual direction should not be confused with psychotherapy or pastoral counseling. Psychotherapy is directed toward solving a psychological problem that interferes with the patient's ability to function as happily or effectively as the patient would like. Once the problem has been addressed to the patient's satisfaction, there is no longer any need for psychotherapy. Psychotherapy is problem oriented and time limited, while spiritual direction can continue indefinitely and is oriented toward enriching the directee's relationship with God. A person may be in spiritual direction and psychotherapy at the same time, but that person's therapist and director should be two different people.

Pastoral counseling addresses life issues such as preparation for marriage, or making a difficult moral decision—for example, whether to have an abortion. Thus, pastoral counseling, unlike spiritual direction but like psychotherapy, is also issue or problem focused and time limited, since the counseling has served its purpose once the issue has been resolved.

No doubt, moral issues will arise from time to time in spiritual direction, but spiritual direction is not the confessional, nor is it a forum for pastoral services such as marriage counseling. A spiritual director may also identify psychological problems that could benefit from professional treatment and suggest that the directee see a psychotherapist. But a director is not the directee's therapist, and so the directee should not see the director primarily as a therapist or pastoral counselor. The director is a spiritual mentor who walks together with the directee on his or her pilgrimage. We now return to the characteristics of a good spiritual director.

St. Teresa of Avila, one of the great mystics of Western Christianity, whose works on contemplative prayer are some of the finest ever written, thought that a director should be experienced in the spiritual life in order to have some practical sense of what he or she is instructing others about, a sound theological education to avoid falling into doctrinal error, and sound common sense.

Joseph Allen, author of *Inner Way* (Grand Rapids: Eerdmans, 1994), a book on Eastern Orthodox spiritual direction, lists five requirements for a good director:

1. "The first is love: not any kind of love, but an openness and readiness to accept another into one's heart. It is a love that takes time and is open to the possible anguish involved." The director must embrace the heavy obligation that he or she assumes in being a spiritual mentor yet simultaneously recognize that only God can bring success to the enterprise. The director must love the directee selflessly in Christ, seeing the relationship to the directee as a gift from God that will benefit the director as much, or more, than it will the directee.

2. A director must recognize that although we invariably fall short of the glory of God, God's glory is greater than our own failures. Allen states that this recognition that humans are sinful must be exercised with love because a director can be destructive if he or she dwells heavily on human imperfections without recognizing that God loves us anyway.

3. A director must have patience, the ability to sit and wait. Spiritual progress proceeds in God's time, not our own.

4. A director must be frank and open (just as the directee must be). Otherwise, the relationship will remain superficial and the results that flow from the relationship will also remain superficial.

5. Finally, detachment is needed to avoid falling into the subjectivity of sentimentality. A director who becomes too involved emotionally with a directee is unlikely to be able to render sound and objective advice.

Just as the director has responsibilities toward the directee, the directee likewise has responsibilities if the relationship is to bear good fruit. These are the characteristics that I personally hope to see in a directee:

1. Openness and honesty. The directee should have a willingness to be as truthful as possible and to share frankly his or her deepest spiritual issues and experiences with the director.

2. Perseverance. The directee should continue working toward spiritual progress even when little progress is apparent. The directee should not change spiritual directors without a compelling reason, although changes are sometimes necessary.

3. Deference to advice. The directee should always treat the director's advice with respect, and if choosing to act contrary to it, should make the reasons known to the director. When a directee is in disagreement regularly with the director, the two may explore whether or not the relationship should continue.

4. Ability to keep confidences. Allen points out, and I agree, that just as a director should treat communications from the directee as confidential, the directee likewise should treat what the director says as confidential. The directee must understand that what the director says in the context of their spiritual direction relationship is meant for them alone. Advice that is sound for one person may be harmful to another. Since a director must address each directee as an individual, the directee must take the advice of the director as a personal and privileged communication.

5. Desire for progress. The most important attribute I look for is the directee's sincere desire to progress in the spiritual life. Spiritual direction is not for those who are half-hearted in their search. It requires an investment on the part of the director that must be warranted by the investment of the directee. This does not mean that the directee must be far advanced before coming to direction, or even that the directee is already on a clear path, but the desire must be present to love God completely and to follow wherever God may lead. Direction is not casual conversation about theological matters. It should relate to a passionate search for what it most important in every human life.

review questions

1. How does psychotherapy differ from spiritual direction? In contrast, how does pastoral counseling differ from spiritual direction?

2. Name five requirements that a good spiritual director should meet.

3. Name five characteristics that the directee should bring to spiritual direction.

4. Why must the directee respect the confidentiality of what the director says, just as the director must respect the confidentiality of what the directee says?

additional questions for discussion

1. What do you think is the most important trait a director must have? Why?

2. What do you think is the most important trait a directee must bring to direction? Why?

3. What reasons might there be that a person's spiritual director should not also be his or her psychotherapist? Can you see any advantages in combining those two roles? If so, what are they?

4. Do you see this group as having the attributes required of a good spiritual director? What are its strengths in this regard? What are its weaknesses?

homework assignment: should this group continue?

Pray about and carefully consider whether you want this group to continue as a forum in which members can provide spiritual direction to one another. The third part of this book will describe how the meetings might be structured to provide for group spiritual direction should the group decide to continue.

Put your thoughts on this question in writing so that you can better share them with the group when it meets again. Being able to express your thoughts in writing might be quite helpful to you in spiritual direction as well. Many people have trouble putting thoughts on paper, but writing often helps to clarify ideas and fix them in the mind. It also provides a "hard copy" of your spiritual questions, experiences, and insights to clarify and fix them in your mind, but also to have a record to review before a session with your spiritual director.

You can practice writing by taking the question "Should the group continue?" and then writing as fast as you can without focusing on exactly what you are putting down on paper. Let the words simply flow out your fingers on to the paper. This is not so-called automatic writing; rather, it is letting your mind express itself without the usual inhibitions and worries—such as, am I being grammatically correct?—that sometimes paralyze the ability to write.

If you do enter spiritual direction later, you will find additional techniques for expressing your spiritual insights and experiences, some perhaps better suited to your temperament.

PART THREE

A REVIEW OF THE PURPOSES OF SPIRITUAL DIRECTION

SPIRITUAL DIRECTION HAS THREE ESSENTIAL ELEMENTS. FIRST, spiritual direction must aid the directee in discerning how God is acting in his or her life and how best to respond to God's action.

Because God desires to bring each and every human being through love into the life of God, the Spirit will be active in each person's life. However, I may fail to be aware of God's action in my life for a variety of reasons. I may, for example, not believe that there is a God who acts in anyone's life, much less my own. Or I may believe that my own life is worth so little, or my conduct has been so sinful, that God, although perhaps willing to expend effort on great saints, would not waste such effort on me. It does seem rather presumptuous that the God of all creation would even notice my existence, much less want to share the divine life with me. But that God is a God who cares passionately about even the least among us is a central message of the Gospels. We would not dare to believe that if God had not revealed this truth to us through Jesus Christ; but once it is revealed, we dare not disbelieve it.

And if God cares about us and wants to bring us to the knowledge of him, then God will do so if we will allow it. Only God can bring us to this knowledge, and so we must allow God to do so if we are going to gain it. That means I must cooperate with the Spirit's work in me if God is to be successful in this effort.

Thus, even if I identify a direction in which God wants to lead me, I must be willing to follow. God will prod but will not compel us toward the goal.

Spiritual direction should help me to identify what God is doing in my life as well as how I might best learn and apply what God is trying to teach me.

Spiritual direction also should make me accountable in my quest to accept the invitation to come to God in love and to open myself to the Spirit's transforming action. Generally, the cornerstone of my attempt to open myself to God will take the form of certain prayer practices, study, and ministry that form a rule of life.

But whether I have a formal rule of life or not, I must still be continually saying yes to the invitation to allow God to bring me to him, and I must continually be open to what God wants to teach me and how God desires to mold me. If there is no one to whom I must report my efforts in this regard, I may soon forget why I have a rule in the first place, or I may let my efforts slip, particularly if it seems that I am making scant progress, or I am even slipping backwards. Spiritual direction helps keep me honest with myself and with God.

Moreover, it is not easy to continue to reaffirm my desire to belong entirely to God and to try to subordinate my will to God's will. Having someone who is understanding and supportive to whom I can relate my struggles, successes, and failures can be an immense blessing. Through a community in which experiences are shared and in which we are supported by prayer and positive reinforcement, we recognize that we are not alone, but are surrounded by a "great cloud of witnesses" who strengthen and encourage us on our journey.

We thus see that spiritual direction can be of great value to the seeker, provided that a wise, compassionate, and compatible spiritual director can be found. Unfortunately, such directors are generally not easy to come by. That is why the group that completed the twelve sessions together might want to remain together to provide group spiritual direction.

what a spiritual direction group is not

Many churches have small groups serving a variety of needs. Some groups provide an opportunity for fellowship over meals, a time simply to enjoy the company of friends, without the constraints of an agenda. Some groups come together to study the Bible; other groups pray for their members or the needs of the wider community. Whatever their purpose, these small groups often provide a greater sense of belonging and community within a larger, perhaps more impersonal, congregation.

A spiritual direction group has one specific purpose that it must always keep in view: to provide spiritual direction for its members. Hopefully, the group will provide its participants with a safe haven and a deep sense of fellowship, but if it fails to provide the key elements of spiritual direction, it is not carrying out the purpose for which it was formed.

There are several pitfalls of which a spiritual direction group should be aware. I discuss some of these now, but the basic question the group must ask itself is this: Are we successfully engaging in spiritual direction as judged by the purposes for spiritual direction?

A spiritual direction group might find itself sidetracked into discussing issues that have little to do with spiritual direction. Someone might bring up the latest concern about the changes the new minister is making in the services, and someone else may want to discuss a resolution that will be voted on at the next general meeting of the denomination. The group, however, does not exist to solve the problems of either the local congregation or the denomination, or even to discuss them. It is not that those issues are inconsequential or uninteresting; rather, they distract the group from its purpose: to provide spiritual direction to its members.

The group must also remember that spiritual direction is distinct from both psychotherapy and pastoral counseling. Psychotherapy deals with a mental or emotional disorder that impairs the sufferer's quality of life. Psychotherapy attempts to cure the disorder or at least enable the patient to experience an acceptable quality of life. Once the disorder has been addressed to the patient's satisfaction, psychotherapy is ended. Pastoral counseling is directed toward "life issues" that involve moral or religious questions, such as whether someone should get a divorce. It also may provide guidance and education, such as in premarital counseling. Once, however, the issue that drew a person to pastoral counseling is resolved, there is no further need for such counseling on that particular issue.

Spiritual direction is a continuing relationship because the Spirit continues to act in our lives and we must constantly renew our yes to God and our openness to him. We will always stand in need of discerning divine action in our lives, determining our response, remaining accountable, and benefiting from others' prayer support.

Unfortunately, there is often no clear line that separates spiritual issues from the emotional disturbances that are the subject matter of psychotherapy or from the life issues that pastoral counseling addresses. If a woman is in an abusive marriage, that will profoundly affect her relationship with God, and the abusive marriage will be intimately associated with what the woman brings to group direction. Likewise, if a man has a serious falling out with his pastor, that will affect his spiritual life.

The group must, therefore, be ready to hear about matters that are outside its avowed purpose but are impacting a member's spiritual progress. At the same time, while the group will be taking such matters into account as it assists in discernment and with prayer, it must avoid straying too far from spiritual direction and must be even more wary of exceeding its competence. Even if a member of the group is credentialed in psychotherapy or pastoral counseling, that individual should refrain from diverting the group from giving spiritual direction. The group's convener, or another member for that matter, could say something like, "The problem you describe sounds like one that should be brought to a pastoral counselor or a therapist. This is not something the group should get involved with, although we love you in Christ and will support you in prayer. How is God present to you in this situation, and do you sense somehow that the Spirit is leading you somewhere even in these difficulties you are having?" Note that the question brings attention back to spiritual direction. The group wants to help the directee to be faithful in interacting with God, even when the group grieves with the directee about the personal crisis the directee is having. Perhaps all the group can, or should, do is support the directee with love and prayer and not attempt direction when the directee is so emotionally stressed. But even so, the group must continue to respect appropriate boundaries and not mistake either its mission or its expertise.

The group may also be tempted to experiment with some new prayer technique that a member is enthused about, or to talk about a book that a member has found extraordinarily helpful. Though the prayer technique may indeed be useful and the book packed with sound wisdom, the group should resist the temptation to become, in effect, a study group, unless it recognizes what it would be doing and intentionally and collectively determines that it is time to change its mission, either temporarily or permanently.

We now examine how meetings of a spiritual direction group might be structured.

the structure of a group meeting

As was the case when the group was studying the material in the twelve sessions, the group must agree on a set of rules that will help (1) the members understand how the group will operate; (2) the meetings run more smoothly and be more productive; (3) the group stay within appropriate boundaries; and (4) the group remain faithful to its goal of providing spiritual direction for all of its members.

The group will probably want to keep many of the rules it already had in place, but certain rules should be reviewed again and intentionally readopted because of their importance. These include the following:

    ✎ Whatever is said in a presentation is to be held in strictest confidence outside the group.

    ✎ All members will make attendance at the meetings a high priority, and any member who must be absent will notify the convener in advance.

    ✎ Persons designated to present must prepare the presentations in advance carefully and prayerfully.

    ✎ Members are to support one another in love and in prayer and not be judgmental.

Obviously, the group can make (or omit) whatever rules members deem appropriate, but openness in presentations, for example, should not be expected unless the group has agreed to a rule of confidentiality.

The purpose of the group is to provide spiritual direction for its members. Spiritual direction generally takes place through a dialogue between the director and the directee, in this case, between the member of the group seeking direction and the other members of the group who, collectively, are acting as the director.

A session might well begin with a moment of silence to give time for all to collect their thoughts and quietly ask God to inspire their thoughts and words to their own benefit and to the benefit of those seeking direction. The convener might close this time of silence with a prayer asking God's guidance and blessing.

The members who will seek direction at the session will have been selected prior to the session with enough advance notice that they might adequately prepare their presentations to the group. My own experience indicates that it takes at least forty-five minutes for each directee/presenter. Thus, if the group meets for an hour and a half, at most two persons per meeting will be able to seek direction.

I will discuss presentations at greater length below. Briefly, in the presentation, the directee relates how God seems to be acting in his or her life, and tells of any new spiritual insights received and about the spiritual issues that are paramount. The presenter concludes by stating prayer requests for the group.

The presenter makes the presentation without interruption. While it may seem desirable to ask questions for clarification during the presentation, doing so breaks the continuity of the presentation and may distract the group from listening carefully and prayerfully to what the presenter is trying to communicate.

Once the presenter is finished with the presentation, there is another moment of silence to give members a chance to reflect on the presentation and to pray for guidance from the Holy Spirit. Always remember that the group must above all else seek to be the faithful instrument of God in helping to clarify what the mind of God is in regard to the directee. What matters most is not what a member of the group would have the directee do or learn, or even what the group as a whole believes is best for the directee, but what God wants the directee to do or learn. Only the directee can make this decision. The group tries in all humility to assist the directee, but it must never impose its will on the directee or mistake its voice for the voice of God.

After the moment of silent reflection and prayer following a presentation, members may ask questions to clarify what the directee meant or to gather more information about the events described or the issues raised. Any advice for the presenter should be offered in a positive, nonjudgmental tone, even if the person offering the advice is convinced that the presenter's conduct is unwise or even sinful.

Members must also keep in mind that the discussion must be directed to the presenter/directee. Although members may refer to their own experiences and issues, these must be relevant to the presentation and be a bona fide attempt to assist the directee, not an effort, made even unconsciously, to refocus the discussion on someone else. The convener must pull the group back to the directee if the discussion begins to wander.

When it appears to the convener that the conversation is becoming repetitive or is flagging, the convener can ask if the presenter is ready for the group to pray. The convener also asks the presenter to restate prayer requests for the group. The presenter may have changes or additions to the initial prayer requests, based on what was said in the discussion. The group members gather around the presenter and pray as they are moved.

Although the convener should suggest closing the discussion when it no longer seems productive, mere silence is not a sign in itself that the discussion is no longer productive. One member, for example, may be pondering an important point, or trying to formulate a question that he believes should be asked. Nor should any member be uncomfortable with remaining silent if she believes she has nothing meaningful to say. Silence also gives the presenter time to reflect on what has already been said. God is often heard most clearly in silence.

The presentation is a central element of group spiritual direction. Naturally, the next question is, Of what do the presentations consist and how are they prepared?

presentations

The following will be addressed to the reader as "you," since it is advice concerning how the reader would make a presentation to the group:

By whatever means seems most appropriate to your temperament, personality, and experience, you will try to communicate the following:

- ✎ the state of your efforts to allow God to act in your life, including any difficulties, successes, and uncertainties encountered in your efforts
- ✎ how God is acting in your life, or how you believe God is failing to act when you think he should be acting
- ✎ any special obstacles or issues with which you are wrestling that you think may have had a substantial impact on your spiritual development
- ✎ any special graces or insights you received since your last presentation to the group
- ✎ what you want the group to pray for on your behalf

Be aware that you need not be accurate in your discernment of your situation, but you must be honest. One task that the group has is to help you find and focus on the real issues.

Although most presentations will be verbal, this need not be the case. One of the most effective presentations I personally have witnessed was through an original painting that depicted the presenter's impression of the current state of her spiritual life.

It would be best if you could keep a daily record or journal of insights and experiences that you believe apply to the five items in the foregoing list. Although not all of these points need be covered in your presentation, at least one of the first four should be included.

A written journal should not be a listing of what you did or did not do; rather, it should reflect your feelings, insights, problems, pain, joy, uncertainty, certainty, and so forth. For example, if you failed to keep your rule of life, your journal should reflect why you failed and how you felt about not keeping it.

Ask yourself questions such as, "What were my most meaningful spiritual experiences or insights, and why were they meaningful?" or, "Have I had a dream in which I thought I heard an important message?" These questions are meant as examples only. If you write, let the writing reflect your true feelings and state of mind, not how you would like to be seen. If you have to think long and hard about what to write, this method of presentation is probably not for you. You should also consider whether you are too concerned about writing a literary work rather than expressing in your own words how God is acting in your life, even if the spelling and grammar leave something to be desired. You should also ask if you are more interested in portraying yourself to the group in a positive light so that members will think well of you rather than giving an honest account of your spiritual struggles.

One word of caution: The group is not a confessional. A member does not have to confess sinful behavior unless genuinely moved to do so. Knowing and intentionally sinful acts should generally be handled according to the member's denominational understanding—for example, confessed to a priest in order to receive sacramental absolution, or confessed in direct appeal to the mercy of God through the merits of Jesus Christ. Someone who is not sure whether a certain behavior is sinful or not should usually view this uncertainty as a matter for pastoral counseling. The emphasis in a spiritual group is not on sin, but on striving to be faithful. As Paul tells us, "We all fall short of the glory of God." The group's emphasis is a positive one on our striving to cooperate with God, not a negative one on the many times we fail. Nothing is more likely to bring the group to a swift end than the expectation that members have to confess even their most secret sins.

Trying to ad lib your presentation is unfair to you and the group, and it significantly diminishes the chance that you will profit from the time and attention devoted to you. At the very least, spend some time to prepare your presentation before the meeting at which you are to present. If you are still at a loss as to what you might share, here are some additional suggestions that might help your presentation.

1. Read from a written journal that you have kept.

2. Bring a picture, color, pattern, or some object that you think illustrates something about your spiritual state, and explain that state and how what you brought reflects it.

3. Write a song, poem, or story, or choose someone else's song, poem, or story that you think illustrates something about your spiritual state, and explain that state and how what you brought reflects it.

4. Relate one or two incidents in your own experience that deeply impressed you and why and how you responded to them spiritually. The incident could even be a dream. It might also be something someone did to or for you or for someone you know, or something you did and how someone responded to it.

When the presentation is finished, the group enters a time of silent reflection and prayer before responding.

the response of the group to a presentation

The convener will indicate when the period of silence has ended, perhaps by saying a short prayer for guidance. The convener will then ask if there are any questions and will make any comments that he or she feels may be appropriate to clarify or to follow up on the points that the presenter has made.

Members of the group may join in, as they feel moved by the Spirit. All must remember that the focus is on the presenter. Remarks and questions should be addressed to and concern the presenter, not other members of the group. No one should feel compelled to speak.

The group may offer questions, observations, suggestions, and opinions in a compassionate and caring manner. Judgments are inappropriate. If someone believes that the presenter is acting wrongly, he or she may suggest this and the reasons for this belief, but never in a harsh, demanding, or judgmental way. Presenters should receive comments in a prayerful, humble, loving, and grateful spirit, and then reflect upon whether the Holy Spirit is trying to lead them through the comments from the group. No presenter is bound to obey a suggestion, but nevertheless should prayerfully weigh any suggestions offered. Ultimately, what decisions the presenter arrives at are between the presenter and God.

In closing the group's response, the convener asks the presenter how the group should pray on his or her behalf.

a time to be born and a time to die

Groups have life cycles like any living organism. A spiritual direction group has a reason to exist so long as it is providing helpful spiritual direction to its members. If, for whatever reason, it can no longer achieve this goal, it should either disband or change its purpose to something else that the members consider mutually beneficial. No one should be afraid to ask whether or not the group should continue or to suggest modifications in the group's procedures that might make meetings more useful and productive to all members.

From time to time, even in a healthy group, members will leave. A death, relocation out of the area, or a change in job or in work schedule, among other reasons, will cause attrition in the group's numbers. At some point, the group may become so small that it needs to reexamine its purpose in light of its diminished numbers and altered group dynamics.

Even two or three people can give direction to one another. But if there are only two or three, that means that a member would make a presentation at almost every meeting if the group met weekly. A smaller group may decide to meet less often, or it may meet more informally with the members first engaging in mutual exploration of how God is acting in their lives and then praying together.

Undoubtedly, at some point in a group's lifetime, someone may ask to join or a member may nominate an acquaintance for membership. Should the group allow new members to join, and if so, under what conditions?

There are at least two strong reasons for not adding members to the group. The first reason is that the group has already been through a formative process by its work with the material in the twelve sessions. A member added later would not have completed this foundational work. Of course, a prospective member could be given the material to read, but this would not be the same thing as having experienced the group's earlier sharing and discussion.

Another reason that adding a new member might be problematic is that the current members know and, presumably, have developed a deep trust in one another. They are willing to share some of the most profound and important experiences of their lives with other members of the group. A new member might not be trusted by the group, and thus her presence could inhibit openness. Conversely, a new member might limit his willingness to share until he feels that the group is safe.

Even so, if every member of the group feels comfortable with the prospective member, and the prospect is willing to read the preparatory material, then he or she might successfully join the group. Ultimately, the group must decide whether or not it feels comfortable adding new members.

A final warning: The group members must never believe that they are the elite of the congregation or an exclusive club from which the less spiritually ambitious are excluded. From their work together they should gain a realistic sense of their sinfulness and their total dependence on God to grow in holiness. From this should come a healthy sense of humility and compassion. For the group to wall itself in is to wall God out. God is found in love, not only the love of members of the group, but of all humanity and, indeed, of all creation. The group is only a spiritual aid. It must never be an end in itself. Only God is the goal and end of all our longing.

AIDS TO THE ADDITIONAL QUESTIONS FOR DISCUSSION

session 1

1. Suppose that through my own efforts alone—perhaps by carefully studying Scripture or by saying certain words over and over again—I could come to a direct knowledge of God. What would this say about God? What would this say about Christianity?

If I could, by my own unaided efforts, come to the knowledge of God, then holiness and the knowledge of God are do-it-yourself jobs. We have no need of Christ to serve as a Way to God; therefore, we have no need of Christianity. It also implies that God can somehow be contained within the constraints of our limited abilities. God would necessarily be finite because our abilities are finite. A limited, finite god is not the God of either Judaism or Christianity.

2. Can you share any experiences that convinced you of your complete dependence on God to come to God?

The answers will necessarily be different for different individuals. But there are some general categories of experiences through which many come to recognize their dependence on God. These include, but are not limited to, a serious illness in which a person recognizes mortality and the inability to control life; a favor granted in response to prayer when the petitioner had thought the situation was hopeless; a recognition of one's weakness, ignorance, and sinfulness with the realization that we cannot come to God unless God permits it and helps us overcome those obstacles we cannot overcome by ourselves; a special experience of God through which is revealed the infinite gulf between God's uncreated Being and our created being.

3. Can you describe an important "God moment" in your life?

Again, we must respect individual experiences. In addition to experiences cited in the answer to question 2, special God experiences might involve a glimpse of God's glory in the beauty of nature; an encounter with God's love as expressed through other human beings; or a special insight given by God during prayer or study.

4. Some religions and philosophies say that a human being can achieve a knowledge of God, or even become God or a god, by performing certain exercises or acquiring secret knowledge without any outside help. Why might such a belief appeal to someone? What problems do you see with it?

This question is similar to question 1, and some of the problems with this view were sketched out there. However, this view is appealing for several reasons. First, it gives us control of our progress toward God rather than forcing us to depend on God. A common human trait is the desire to retain control. Second, it means that we can come to God at our own pace and in ways that we might find more comfortable than the ways in which God would lead us. Third, it allows us to feel special, people apart from the herd, because we have secret knowledge that places us above the rest of humanity. We are the "initiated." This is vastly different from Christianity, in which all persons are equal before Christ and all are invited to the wedding banquet of God's kingdom.

5. God is a mystery in the sense that God cannot be understood by using our natural mental powers no matter how long or hard we study. What other mysteries were mentioned in the reading? Are you concerned that many truths of our faith are mysteries? Does the fact that we are dealing with mysteries create problems with describing our faith to others? How do you address this problem?

Virtually anything having to do with God and God's relation to humanity is a mystery; that is, it lies beyond our natural powers of understanding. If we can fully describe or understand some idea with our natural abilities, then that idea is not God. We are, in a real sense, looking for God in the darkness of faith rather than in the light of our intellects. This means that, pressed to describe God to an inquirer, we cannot do so without resorting to incomplete and often unsatisfying descriptors like all-good, all-powerful, creator of the universe, and so on. We each construct images of God in our minds because that is how our minds operate. We need something to grab hold of that enables us to relate to God. This is one reason that God gave us the incarnation. Through Jesus Christ, both human and divine, we can learn more about God through observing the man Jesus. But even then, we do not see God directly. Just as we learn more about God through learning more about Christ, so should we pray and try, by God's grace, to behave in ways that will allow others to see God through us as we see God through Christ.

session 2

1. If you were God, how would you treat someone who deliberately disobeyed you? If you are or were a parent, how do or would you treat a child who deliberately disobeyed you? Are your two responses consistent with one another?

If we consider God as Father, do we consider him to be a

loving Father, one who has all the attributes of an ideal human father? Do human fathers generally destroy their offspring or disown them for disobedience?

2. Are there sins—that is, obstacles to union with God—so great that they cannot be overcome? If so, describe such a sin. If not, why not?

Jesus talks about only one sin that cannot be forgiven, which is the sin of demonizing the Holy Spirit. If we are willing to recognize God as good and humbly ask for forgiveness in the name of Christ, God will forgive us. If we consider God to be the devil, then asking God for forgiveness is a mockery.

3. What do you think is the primary obstacle to God's transforming grace in us; that is, what is the most common sin?

Opinions may differ, but I think that pride is the primary sin, whereby we insist on controlling our own destiny rather than submitting ourselves to God's love and transforming grace. Pride is an obstacle to being open with God and to accepting God's guidance in our lives. In a sense, we attribute to ourselves powers that only God has.

4. If God had chosen to do so, could God have created us so that we could not sin? If God had done so, would we also have had free will and the ability to love?

Only beings who have free choice can sin. God could have created us sinless by depriving us of the ability to choose freely. But if we cannot freely sin, neither can we freely love. The price of being able to love is the ability to choose wrongly, to sin.

session 3

1. Can you give additional examples of rituals by which something or someone is consecrated?

Christians may consecrate missionaries for mission work before sending them off, or may consecrate the buildings in which they worship with special rituals.

2. Is consecration unique to Judaism and Christianity? What other religious groups might honor some rite of consecreation?

Almost all the religions of the world have some form of consecration, whether it be setting someone apart for priestly or shamanic duties, or creating certain space as sacred for worship.

3. Even if we study the Scriptures and pray for guidance, we cannot always be sure what God wants us to do in every situation. With which of our choices do you believe God is most concerned? Do you believe that God "micromanages"?

Some do believe that God is responsible for even the smallest details of our lives. I personally believe that God gives us a great deal of latitude, consistent with giving us free will. To learn, we must experiment. Sometimes being able to make mistakes is the only way we can learn. God does, I believe, try to guide us toward choices that will make it easier for us to come into union with him. Some of these "God events" are more obvious than others. As some wit once said, "Coincidence is God's way of acting anonymously."

4. Thomas Merton, a noted Roman Catholic monastic and writer, said that he did not know if what he did pleased God, but he was sure that his desire to please God pleased God. Do you agree with this statement? If we are not sure what choice God wants us to make in a particular situation, how should we act? Should we refuse to act until we are certain of God's will?

To refuse to act is to act. If we waited to act until we were certain what God wanted of us, we would be paralyzed most of the time. We do the best we can in the circumstances of our lives. I am convinced that many people are living lives of heroic

holiness, attempting to be faithful to God's will as they understand it under difficult conditions. God does not demand that
we succeed, only that we be faithful.

session 4

*1. Have you ever experienced pain or loss because you acted as
your conscience dictated?*

The answer, obviously, will differ from individual to individual. My suspicion is that there are few Christians who have not
had to make at least some choices that would have been made
differently if a matter of moral conscience or fidelity to God were
not involved.

2. Which lesson of the cross is most attractive to you? Why?

My own choice is that the cross demonstrates the lengths to
which God is willing to go to bring us to him. Others may have
different choices. Explain why you feel most drawn to a particular lesson of the cross.

*3. Christ's love was unconditional and unselfish. He wanted to
bring every human being into the Kingdom, and he had no
thought of personal reward in doing so. Is human love usually
this way? Is our love of God unconditional and unselfish?
Would we love God as much if we did not want the reward of
heaven or if we did not fear the punishment of hell? Do we really want to share the joys of heaven with our worst enemies?*

There are "politically correct" answers to these questions, but
if most Christians are honest, they will admit that getting into
heaven or avoiding hell is a powerful motive in their actions.
God, however, loves us unselfishly and unconditionally.
Normally, we love those who appreciate our love and respond
positively to it and avoid people who do not appeal to us or who
we know dislike us. But if we are going to love others as we have

first been loved by God, then we have to be willing to lay down our lives, if need be, so that even our most bitter enemy could come into the Kingdom. This is how we were first loved by Christ, after all—while we were still sinners and enemies of God.

session 5

1. Would you try to obey God even if you did not believe in life after death? Why or why not?

My own view is that if people did not believe that there is life after death, most would not try to obey God. Why should they? They will not be around after they die for God either to punish or to reward them. If this life is all there is, then we might as well get as much from it as we can. We can say that God will reward good people and punish evil people in this life, but experience does not always seem to bear this out.

2. Atheists think of life as a mere accident of nature having no real purpose or goal. Some Christians think of life as a time to test us to see if we are worthy to enter heaven. Others believe that life is a school in which we are to learn wisdom and love. What is your own view of the purpose of life?

I favor the view that life is a school. Loving parents try to teach their children what they should know in order to realize their full potential.

3. How would you like the other members of the group to pray on your behalf? Ask the group to pray for you, and let each member voice a prayer in his or her own words for your intention.

Each person will have his or her special prayer intentions. Be open both in revealing what you would like from God and in praying for others. Do not judge whether what someone wants is right or wrong.

session 6

1. Identify one or more possibilities for your own spirituality. Which seems most in line with your temperament as well as your present interests and circumstances?

You may be especially attracted to some truth of the faith, such as the incarnation; or an event in Christ's life, such as his raising of Lazarus; or a particular ministry, such as administration or healing. You might also be attracted to the life of a particular saint, like Benedict or Francis of Assisi.

2. Name a Christian you particularly admire. What is that individual's spirituality? Is it a spirituality to which you feel attracted?

One might name, for example, Mother Teresa, with her compassion for the poor and the oppressed; or Albert Schweitzer, with his missionary medical work. Most of us have admired and perhaps tried to imitate a great Christian whose works and example inspired us.

3. In what ways did Jesus exhibit the following spiritualities: a spirituality of poverty? a spirituality of teaching? a spirituality of compassion toward the suffering? What are some other spiritualities you can identify in Christ?

Spirituality of poverty: "Foxes have dens and the birds of the air have nests, but the Son of Man has nowhere to lay his head." Jesus is never seen seeking self-enrichment or asking anyone to pay for his services. Spirituality of teaching: Jesus is constantly teaching both the crowds and his disciples. Spirituality of compassion: Jesus' many healings attest to his compassion. At times, as with the son of the widow of Nain, he had compassion on someone who did not even have to ask for it. Other spiritualities: healing ministry, attention to children, anointing by the Holy Spirit, and so on.

session 7

1. Which form of thought do you lean toward, verbal or pictorial? Does the answer depend on what you are thinking about? Does it change from time to time?

The answer will vary from person to person. It is important to remember that one mode of thought is not better or worse than another, just different.

2. Which of the meditative exercises did you find easier? What obstacles to meditating did you have in each exercise? How might these be lessened?

The most common obstacle to meditation is distraction. The mind tends to wander or want to focus on some issue unrelated to the meditation. The more a person tries to fight distractions, the more he or she interferes with prayer, because the fight itself becomes distracting and causes the person to focus on the distraction as well. Sometimes it helps to ignore distractions, just as we ignore traffic noise from the street outside or static in a phone conversation. Let the distraction be background noise.

3. What forms of inspiration for meditation do you think would work best for you? Have you actually engaged in periods of meditation before but did not know it was called meditation?

Obviously, individuals will have differing answers. Some prefer to use their senses as a springboard to meditation, others a Scripture reading, others an inspirational picture, and so on. Most people, once they have been told what meditation is, realize that they have meditated frequently in the past.

session 8

1. In addition to memory, reason, and will, humans have a characteristic that seems utterly unique to humanity: self-

consciousness. We not only know, but also are aware that we know. We recognize ourselves as distinct individuals. Another example of a characteristic apparently unique to human beings is the ability to appreciate music. What are some other characteristics that appear to be unique to human beings?

Even lower animals seem to have memory, will, and some minimal ability to reason. Anyone who owns a cat or a dog will have no trouble agreeing with this. The degree to which lower animals are self-conscious is a matter of controversy, although it would not be surprising if animals did have some minimal sense of self, although not to the degree that self-consciousness occurs in humans. Moral sense may be a peculiarly human trait. Another is a sense of humor. Perhaps you can think of others.

2. What are the implications of self-consciousness for spiritual growth? For example, if we were not self-conscious, would we be able to recognize the difference between good and evil? Would we be aware that someday each of us must die?

Self-consciousness does not necessarily imply a moral conscience, since there are so-called sociopaths who apparently have no conscience at all. However, if we could not distinguish between good and evil, we would, presumably, always choose what we thought would bring us the greatest immediate pleasure. If we did not know good and evil, how could we sin, since we would not recognize disobedience to God as any worse than obedience to God? Our knowledge that we will someday die should give immediacy to trying to live as we believe we should in order to accomplish those goals for which we have been placed here.

3. How is faith defined as "accepting a statement as true because God has revealed it" different from faith as complete trust in God? Can we have one form of faith without the other? Which form of faith is more important for spiritual growth? Why?

We can believe in theological statements without applying them in our lives. It is hard to have absolute trust in God without acting on that trust. If we sincerely believe that God has called us into union with him and will bring us to that union if we will allow it, that trust can help us relinquish control of our lives to God. A desire to do things our way rather than God's way may indicate a lack of confidence in God's love for us.

session 9

1. What signs lead me to believe that God is active in my life?

Each person will have a different story. God acts with an individual in ways suited to that individual. God gives us the gifts we need, not necessarily the ones we want.

2. If God calls every human being into union with him, why do so many seem unaware of this divine invitation? What means could we use to make others more aware of the invitation to know God?

God often speaks with a "still, small voice," and the numerous distractions of the world often drown out that voice. One person may be so convinced that he knows what God is like that he misses God calling to him in a way that is inconsistent with his beliefs. Another person may have been so wounded by circumstances or tragedy that she cannot believe that a loving God really cares about her.

3. If I sense that God seems to be calling me to some unusually difficult activity, what means can I use to determine if that call is truly from God?

Among the means of which you can take advantage are (1) to pray that God will confirm the call and not allow you to be deceived; (2) to test the call by consultation with trusted spiritual friends and your minister; and (3) to study the Scripture to see if the call is consistent with the gospel.

session 10

1. In what ways is being part of a faith community likely to help in the practice of your rule? What difficulties does one face trying to grow spiritually in isolation?

Jesus said that where two or three are gathered together in his name, he is with them. Generally, greater spiritual power and energy are exercised through a group than by an individual. Having to be accountable to others will encourage fidelity to the rule, but receiving prayer support and encouragement from others will also be an aid. Being able to confide in a group may also help a person discern if the rule is an appropriate one for that individual or what changes need to be made to make it more effective. A "lone ranger" is less likely to be faithful in keeping the rule, since there is no accountability and less help to discern how God is acting, or wants to act, in his or her life.

2. Taking care of your health, for example, by exercising a specific amount during the week, can also be part of your rule of life. Why can such seemingly secular activities as exercise reasonably form part of a spiritual rule?

We are embodied individuals, and our bodies are instruments of service to God and others. We therefore need to treat our bodies with respect and keep them as well as possible so that we can use them most effectively in service and prayer.

3. Have you identified your spirituality yet? If so, what is it, and why does it appeal to you?

The answers will vary according to the individual.

session 11

1. Name someone who was especially influential in forming you spiritually. What characteristics did this person have that were helpful in your formation?

The answers will vary, but most Christians have had someone who has had a special impact on their spiritual growth. Many of these influential persons may not even be aware of the positive impact they have had on others' lives. Possible influences include a relative, a prominent contemporary Christian, a saint who lived some time ago, a minister, or a teacher.

2. A spiritual director must be compassionate, recognizing that all human beings are imperfect. However, would you prefer a director who called attention to what he or she thought was wrongful behavior on your part, or a director who was nonjudgmental and who let you form your own conclusions about what was right and wrong for you?

Some people want a director who does not "pull punches," but most people prefer the nonjudgmental approach. The latter should always be the approach of the group toward its members.

3. Do you feel that this group has given you spiritual direction as you have proceeded through the sessions? Would you feel comfortable allowing this group to continue as your spiritual director(s) once the sessions are finished?

This is a question that the group must discuss as it decides whether it wishes to continue as a spiritual direction group.

session 12

1. What do you think is the most important trait a director must have? Why?

Some may feel that experience in spiritual life is most important so that the director will be able to relate personally to what the directee is experiencing. Others may stress a compassionate, understanding nature. Still others may emphasize the ability to keep confidences. Expect a variety of answers.

2. What do you think is the most important trait a directee must bring to direction? Why?

My own opinion is that the two most important traits a directee must bring are a sincere desire to be found by God and an openness in talking about his or her spiritual life. However, there are other views that can be supported with good reasons.

3. What reasons might there be that a person's spiritual director should not also be his or her psychotherapist? Can you see any advantages in combining those two roles?

One danger in combining both roles is that either the director or directee, or both, will see the director primarily as therapist and not be able to deal as effectively with spiritual direction; or if the therapist is seen as spiritual director, the therapy may suffer. There may be confusion as to which role the director is playing at any given time. A doctor/patient relationship is different from a director/directee relationship, and the characteristics needed for success in the former will not necessarily bring success in the latter. One possible advantage of combining therapist and director relationships is that curing psychological pathologies may enable the directee to make better progress spiritually.

4. Do you see this group as having the attributes required of a good spiritual director? What are its strengths in this regard? What are its weaknesses?

The responses will vary from group to group. Members of the group must be willing to look honestly at their feelings about the group and its potential as a spiritual direction group. If the members cannot be honest in a positive and compassionate manner, then the odds of the group successfully becoming a spiritual direction group are not good.